Should We Burn Babar?

SHOULD WE BURN BABAR?

*Essays on Children's Literature
and the Power of Stories*

Herbert Kohl

The New Press
New York

Published in the United States by The New Press, New York
Distributed by W. W. Norton & Company, Inc., New York

Established in 1990 as a major alternative to the large, commercial publishing houses, The New Press is the first full-scale nonprofit American book publisher outside of the university presses. The Press is operated editorially in the public interest, rather than for private gain; it is committed to publishing in innovative ways works of educational, cultural, and community value that, despite their intellectual merits, might not normally be commercially viable. The New Press's editorial offices are located at the City University of New York.

Book design by Ann Antoshak
Production management by Kim Waymer
Printed in the United States of America

95 96 97 98   9 8 7 6 5 4 3 2 1

To Mark Weiss,
whose infectious spirit and dedication to all children is an inspiration

Contents

A few years ago, during a visit to a high school, I sat in on a class discussion on violence in the school. The discussion was loud and animated. Every student had a story to tell and there was a lot of competition for attention. The teacher, in order to focus the discussion, silenced the class and made a plea for the students to tell their stories briefly and "get to the point." He did it in order to be able to fit the discussion into the fifty-minute period they had together and to be able to come to some conclusion before the bell. However, instead of focusing the class discussion, the students fell silent. The stories they had to tell were their point. They wanted a moment to share their distress in a personal and intimate way. They wanted to be heard, not to summarize. And they and their teacher knew that the only sensible conclusion to the discussion would have been to continue it to the next time and let it take up the space in the curriculum that the seriousness of the issue demanded.

The teacher, who had invited me to observe his class, was a caring and passionate person. He poured his life into teaching and was annoyed with himself for having shut down the conversation. I remember his comments to me after the class. He said that the climate at the school and in the world of education was getting to him. He felt pressured to rush the students to conclusions, to show increments of learning, to meet preset objectives, to establish goals, and to test acheivement—anything but tell stories and have conversations. And yet, in his judgement, stories and unrushed conversations about serious issues were at the center of his most effective teaching. He was concerned that his students' lives, their stories and dreams, were being dumped, and that he was being dragged along by the mechanical demands of corporate-driven twenty-first-century learning and becoming a less effective and caring teacher.

Because of this and similar experiences I have had observing schools, I have been worrying about the abandonment of stories as powerful tools of teaching and learning. My concern led to the particular configuration of essays included in this collection. In them I hope to show how important good tales are for the development of the self and how dangerous some stories can be when they are presented as history and used to distort the truth. I also want to illustrate how each school year can be considered a story and how the telling of that tale is a valuable form of educational reflection. Moving beyond the classroom, I want to plea for the creation of a radical children's literature that projects hope and provides youngsters with the sense that social forms are constructed by people and therefore that the world can be made into a finer, more caring place. Finally, in story form, I intend to present the neglected history of progressive education in the United States and reaffirm the struggle within schools for economic and social democracy.

All of the essays in this collection are about the power of stories. The first essay, "Should We Burn Babar?," centers on the question of what we should do with a children's book that has achieved the status of a classic and yet is patently racist, colonialist, and sexist. It wrestles with the question of censorship which is a tempting, though equally troubling, way to deal with a text whose content is objectionable.

The second essay, "The Politics of Children's Literature: Rosa Parks and the Story of the Montgomery Bus Boycott," is about the misrepresentation of African American struggles for equality in school textbooks. It shows how the story of Rosa Parks, which is also the story of community-based struggle against segregation, has been turned into a tale of individual frustration, thereby defusing its political content.

"In Support of Radical Children's Literature," the third essay, is an attempt to answer George Orwell's question about the absence of good radical children's literature. It is an attempt to define what radical children's literature might look like, provide some examples of it, and suggest ways in which people might go about creating this genre.

The fourth essay, "Wicked Boys and Good Schools," provides three different takes on Pinocchio, using the story of the mischievous puppet as the basis for a discussion of the role of stories in education. It also speculates on the value of looking at a school year as a story itself.

The final essay, "The Good Old Days. I Was There. Where Was They?," is itself a story. It is a fictional acount of a teaching family. The essay is an attempt to establish, in condensed story form, that progressive educational ideas are as old as American democracy. The tale shows the conflicts that have existed throughout the history of our nation between education for democracy and education that institutionalizes privilege.

There are many people with whom I discussed the texts and ideas in this book and I thank them all for taking the time to listen and comment. This includes friends, students, and all of the people at The New Press who made this book possible. In particular, and once again, I thank my wife, Judy, for providing the tough and caring criticism I need to craft my work.

I hope this collection of stories about stories moves people to tell their own tales and listen to the tales of their children's and their students' lives and dreams.

INTRODUCTION

Jack Zipes

Should We Burn Babar? is very much in keeping with Herb Kohl's other provocative books, which deal forthrightly with the politics of education and his experiences in American schools. He does not mince his words or disguise his politics. As one of the foremost progressive educators in America, Kohl seeks to spell out the contradictions that plague children, teachers, parents, and schools and that prevent the development of literacy and learning in a communal way. The analysis of different children's books in *Babar* is not a traditional academic study but is set in the context of ideological struggles in schools and communities, in which Kohl himself has participated.

When Kohl talks about *Babar* and *Pinocchio* and interprets the negative elements of colonization and sexism in these works, he does not develop his critique in abstraction, nor does he intend to rid America of these stories because they are harmful to children. On the contrary, he introduces the opinions of children and teachers and incorporates them in his own analysis. In this way, Kohl focuses on the need for greater discussion and awareness of how the ideologies of these remarkable books affect young readers.

All of Kohl's observations are based on historical research and a desire to understand why we are drawn to particular aesthetics and ideologies at different stages of our lives. In one essay, Kohl examines the myths about Rosa Parks and the Montgomery Bus Boycott and reconstructs the story in a way that is more consonant with facts and with the strength and dignity of the African American community. In another essay, he seeks to develop a radical children's literature—gleaned from the works of Geoffrey Trease, Virginia Hamilton, and others—that enables children to grasp the complete social picture of a problem and that doesn't mislead them into believing that single leaders with charisma can change the world. In a third essay, he uses his own fictional history of public education in the United States as an example of how it is possible to reclaim a progressive tradition and keep innovation and experimentation alive in our public schools at a time when they are threatened by privatization, commercialization, and greater standardization.

Throughout the book, Kohl questions why we often produce and teach children's literature that avoids talking about America's social problems. Moreover, he shows how the aesthetics of the most common and classical books for children are related to regressive practices in schools and libraries and maintained by publishers.

The crisis of children's literature, which is also a crisis of education in America, comes alive in Kohl's book. He does not preach but raises questions and stimulates the imagination. His voice also represents the concerns of many educators who are promoting a literature that speaks out in the interests of children and communities and addresses their concerns in an incisive and engaging manner.

Stories, Kohl maintains, are a means to convey power to children and to enable them to take control of their own lives. Stories can also be used to deprive children from seeing their world as it is. In *Should We Burn Babar?* Kohl's reports, observations, and insights open vistas to new possibilities in children's literature and education. Reading Herb Kohl in critical times is like taking a journey with a wise and sincere storyteller whose tales illuminate the truth about the underlying crisis in children's literature. At the end of the journey, we know that there are no quick solutions, but at least we can see where we are and what we must do if children's literature in America is to develop both its own integrity and the integrity of our children.

Should We Burn Babar?
Questioning Power in Children's Literature

The Charming Babar

When I was about five or six my mother or aunt bought a copy of *Babar the Elephant* along with a recording of the book on three 78 rpm records. They read me the book over and over, and I listened to the records endlessly. I remember crying when Babar's mother was killed, being delighted that the Rich Lady was willing to take Babar in and civilize him, feeling happy for Babar when he returned home and was made king, and wishing him the most wonderful time when he and Celeste got married and flew off in an air balloon to have adventures. I loved the book, identified with Babar, and found an abiding affectionate place for him in my heart. The illustrations made Babar seem friendly, socialized—a child-adult. I remembered him leaning on the fireplace, dressed in a three-piece suit and conversing with the Rich Lady's friends, telling them about his life in the wilds, and also him holding a piece of chalk in his trunk doing arithmetic at a chalkboard. The thought of *Babar* evoked memories of moments in my childhood when my aunts and my mother cared for me and indulged my wishes the way the Rich Lady did for the errant elephant.

Recently I decided to reread *Babar* and other children's books that had been part of my growing up. I had revisited some of these books in the early 1970s when my children were very young. My wife and I read to them every night and occasionally shared books we loved as children with our children. My current concern with *Babar* and other classics has derived from work I have been doing in California with Native American children and their parents, and in New York City with high school students. One youngster I work with at home in California is currently engaged in a battle over *The Little House on the Prairie* series. As moving as that "classic" might seem to European American readers, it is offensive to Native American people who are portrayed in the books as barely human savages. The subtext of the books is the conquest of the prairies, and, though the series' personal tales of White settlers are beautifully rendered, its dehumanization of the Native Peoples whose lands are being stolen makes it painful reading. This is especially so for Daniel and a few of his friends who live on a reservation and whose families have experienced similar thievery within living memory of the tribal elders. Daniel is being punished in school for rejecting the book and refusing to answer questions about it. He is also being supported in this resistance by the tacit approval of older people in the community who correctly believe that the local schools do not serve their children well.

In New York a number of high school students I have had occasion to talk with have expressed passionate pleas for exposure to literature they can relate to as well as equally strong objections to the literature they were exposed to as children. Their vehement anger at books and tales such as *Dr. Doolittle, Snow White and the Seven Dwarves,* and *The Little Prince* surprised me. They were not merely asking for the inclusion of texts that represented the stories of African Americans and Latinos, but for the wholesale reconsideration of what is considered appropriate reading for young people.

My inclination was to sympathize with these young people, yet I felt uneasy about throwing out all the books that I read or that were read to me as a child. Hence the question of dear *Babar*. Was *Babar* so offensive that it should be eliminated? Or so powerful an influence that it was dangerous to young children? More generally, if literature has an influence on children's behavior, then the classics may present a problem for parents and teachers if their content portrays, sanctions, and even models inequity. What to do about kings and princesses? About the triumph of the strong and the mocking of the weak? About the glorification of wealth and the sanction of "deserved" poverty? About the portrayal of some people as civilized and others as savage? Should books that represent these antidemocratic sentiments be a major part of our children's earliest repertoire of stories and tales, or should we avoid purchasing them and sharing them with our children? Should we burn books like *Babar*?

I decided to take another, closer, look at *Babar* and ask myself whether I thought burning *Babar* could in any way be in the interest of young people. In particular, I decided to analyze the way in which power is represented in that story, since power relationships in literature reveal the politics of both the story and, frequently, the author. Power relationships also provide examples and models for children of social and moral behavior. I chose *Babar* as my exemplar because I liked the book and want to believe that its charm overrides any offensive attitudes it embodies. In addition, the book reaches tens, if not hundreds, of thousands of children every year. It has been continuously in print in English since 1933, and has reached such a level of popularity that there are dolls, cups, mugs, T-shirts, bibs, sheets, and pillowcases all displaying and celebrating the elephant king. In addition there is an innocence to *Babar* that must be seductive for young children.

Jean de Brunhoff, the creator of *Babar*, is a master narrator. His text ignores transitions. One event happens after another with no explanations; no motives or causes are revealed, no actions justified or excused—events are just told. The reader is swept along without questioning any of the premises of the story. Babar's mother is killed. The Rich Lady gives Babar her purse. Celeste and Arthur run away and immediately find Babar. That's it—scene after scene, so that the book reads almost like an animated cartoon in which events follow so quickly after each other that there is no time for reflection or examination. *Babar* is compelling that way, and effective because it draws the reader on, or, more accurately, it draws the listener on. It is a book that begs a lap or a small circle of children looking up at the illustrations. The book is a perfect model of the genre of illustrated children's books meant to be read aloud. And, if offensive, it is a masterpiece of propaganda, since it is easy to accept the whole of it unquestioned and even to internalize some of the attitudes and ideas it presents.

I want to question the text of *Babar* in a way that children don't, and speculate on the potential effects of this apparently innocent and charming tale. The first and simplest question I'd like to ask is: Who has the power in *Babar*? Who makes the decisions in the story? Who is obeyed and tells the other characters what to do? And how is power distributed among the characters in the text?

In *Babar* the power is with people and not animals. The story begins when a hunter shoots Babar's mother and tries to trap Babar. Next we find Babar lost in a city, where a Rich Lady takes him under her wing.

The hunter is dressed in full colonial regalia, pith helmet and all. He has a double-barreled shotgun and is faceless. All we see of him is his heavy, imposing body, the back of his head, and the side of his face. He is an impersonal force, and his hidden face makes it impossible for children to identify him with the other, more benevolent, humans in the book. In particular the contrast between him and the "very rich Rich Lady," who has a kind though slightly imperious face and elaborate and elegant clothes, is enormous. She is personal—she even does setting-up exercises with Babar in the morning—whereas the hunter and his bullet are one, anonymous and indifferent to the fate of elephants.

Babar flees the hunter but is putty in the hands of the Rich Lady. Resistance to the temptations to lose his elephant nature seems foreign to him. The Rich Lady dresses Babar like a person, teaches him human eating and bathing habits, and educates him like a person. Babar seems to welcome all of this. At the same time the reader is never told what motivates the hunter, the Rich Lady, or Babar. People power works mysteriously and unambiguously in the story.

The Rich Lady has money, lots of it. The source of her wealth is unclear. (Maybe it has to do with hiring hunters to trap and kill elephants?) It is clear that in the book the use of money and the earning of it are two totally different matters, and that it is perfectly normal and in fact delightful that some people have wealth they do not have to work for. Babar becomes one of them.

Babar is impressed both by the ways of the city (especially by the clothes of two elegant men) and with the fact that the Rich Lady feels perfectly comfortable giving him her purse to buy himself some proper clothes. I remember loving the scene where Babar goes into a department store and rides up and down on the elevator until he is chased out and told that he must do his shopping. I always wanted to do that, but my mother was always too busy to ride the elevator just for the fun of it. I also remember giggling at Babar trying his clothes on and can still remember the part on my records where the narrator describes Babar's buying clothes. The whole business of Babar's getting peopleized was an intriguing idea to me as a child, and though we didn't have any pets I could imagine dressing up a dog or cat and pretending that I was the Rich Lady and my pet was Babar. At the same time, rereading the book, I remember being tired as a child of being dressed up by adults and admired for doing what they wanted me to do rather than what I wanted to do. I loved Babar and must have hated him a bit too. However, as an adult I am bothered by his malleability and the good humor with which he jumps into becoming a well-dressed rich person-like elephant. I know if I read *Babar* with a class of young children I would certainly bring up that issue.

In the story there seem to be no limits to the Rich Lady's generosity. "She gives him whatever he wants," including an automobile. She also has a learned professor give Babar lessons, and she shows Babar off to her distinguished friends, whom Babar tells "all about life in the great forest." The only thing she does not give him is a map and food for the journey home, even though we see Babar looking forlornly out the window and thinking of the elephants he left behind.

The Rich Lady has no husband in the story. She does have distinguished friends and is clearly of a better class than the floorwalker and the other shopkeepers Babar encounters. The source of her power is her money—we know little else about her.

The role of money in the story points up the powerlessness of Babar. He does what he is told, is as passive as a paper doll and as uncomplaining. It is hard to imagine Babar opposing the Rich Lady or hurting her feelings. Whenever there is a question of Babar's doing something that might be disagreeable to her, he agonizes over it. And when he finally decides to return to the world of elephants for a temporary visit, he does it with her consent. Is all of this because of her money and its power over Babar?

In *Babar* the reader learns that there are different classes of people and the Rich Lady is of the better (that is richer) class and that elephants are not as good as people, but might be if they imitate people. Was I aware of those distinctions as a child? Did I learn to admire the rich from reading the book? Did I also learn about the inferiority of creatures from the jungle (people included)? I can't be sure, but I do think that from my early reading I got the impression that people who served the rich weren't as good as the rich.

Yet I got the opposite impression from my neighborhood and home. In fact my grandparents were deeply involved in union activities and talked about the rich and the bosses as if they were morally, intellectually, and otherwise evil and deficient. My reading contradicted my family's attitudes, and, since I never met a rich person, I was left with a certain puzzlement. I believe my reading made me feel that my grandparents might not have been telling the full truth about the rich; nevertheless, I didn't believe everything I read. *Babar*, as a story, was just that: one tale to weigh against both the other stories I heard and read, and my own experience. And my experiences with people, even as a six-, seven-, and eight-year-old, told me that people just aren't as generous as the Rich Lady was without ultimately wanting something back. I suspected the Rich Lady and still do. But I didn't dislike her and wouldn't mind running into someone like her who would take a fancy to me on my own terms.

I believe *Babar* set me to musing on trust and wealth but don't believe any conclusions resulted from those thoughts. The book showed me one way things might work. Other books and the world showed me other ways. The Rich Lady didn't do me any harm. However, the image of transforming one's life and fundamentally changing, which I knew from other fairy tales as well, did stay with me. Perhaps what I held dearest about Babar was his ability to recover from his mother's death and go on to make a life for himself. The loss of a mother, which I had not experienced, was, in the charged atmosphere of my growing up at the end of the Depression and during World War II, symptomatic of all the losses people were experiencing in my neighborhood. One appeal of that cute little elephant story was that it began with a loss and then went on to show that life was still possible.

Babar's story centers on the tension between his elephant world and the world to which the Rich Lady introduces him. There are many questions that can be raised about her and her wealth. For example, how does the Rich Lady maintain her fortune? Is she safe from thieves and selfish relatives? What might she do if Babar turned out to be dishonest? Had Babar ever thought about taking her money and running?

There are several ways to look at the Rich Lady's generosity with her money. One is as a way to buy power, protection, and an amusing life. From this view she is seen as an extension of the patriarchy, a product of capitalism and colonialism who maintains power by buying it. A totally different way of looking at the Rich Lady's role is as a caring and sympathetic woman who is providing an alternative to the patriarchy. She introduces generosity and kindness into a male-dominated world, as represented by the hunter and the image of the city as a difficult place to know without friends. There are elements in the story that support this view. She does nothing to exploit Babar (except perhaps to show him off to her friends), and she lets him go home when he wants. Perhaps she can even be interpreted as the Jane Addams of her time, a social worker who welcomes immigrant elephants and helps them settle into their new land.

Both ways of looking at the Rich Lady can be supported by the text, and in fact there is no contradiction in her being a kind person who, while benefiting from her family's exploitation of others, does not herself exploit others. Under this interpretation, the Rich Lady maintains her power through money, but builds other, more humane and affectionate relationships through the generous use of that wealth. This lesson on the use of wealth can even be appealed to in support of having children read the book.

However, there is a third interpretation of the Rich Lady's generosity that has been suggested to me. Under that view, the Rich Lady is very insecure in the world of people and immediately finds herself through contact with the innocence and purity of Babar. They are kindred souls, and so she takes him in as a member of the family, perhaps as a foster son. In that way, her relationship with Babar helps her maintain power over her feelings and acquire strength to overcome the alienation she feels in the world of people. This suggestion is intriguing, though we do meet four of the Rich Lady's people friends in the book.

Toward the middle of the story Babar finds his cousins Celeste and Arthur, who have run away from the forest. It is not clear whether they had Babar in mind when they set out on their adventure, but it is pretty clear that life in the wild was not enough for them. The attractions of civilization were becoming seductive for the young generation of the elephant world.

Babar promptly takes to civilizing his cousins. Through acquiring the accoutrements of civilization and access to the Rich Lady's purse, he has assumed power over other, less fortunate elephants. After kissing his cousins hello, the first thing Babar does is introduce them to the benefits of wealth. He takes them to the department store and buys them expensive clothes. He has learned his lessons thoroughly and presumably still has access to the Rich Lady's purse, for he treats his cousins quite well. They seem delighted to be transformed into imitations of people. The three of them even go to a pastry shop and have some sweets.

The story moves on relentlessly from Babar's civilizing Arthur and Celeste. Babar has been so taken in by people-ways that he does the job of recruiting for them. This is one form of colonization: seducing some members of the group into letting them proselytize for you.

Arthur's and Celeste's mothers come to fetch them from the city, and Babar decides to take them all back to the forest. Before he leaves he packs his trunk with all of his possessions—his hat and tie and walking cane and toiletries and box of bonbons. He has no desire to revert to kind and be just an elephant again. As they leave, the Rich Lady stands on the balcony of her house and sadly wonders, "When shall I see *my* little Babar again?" (italics mine). She has it right: by the time she is done civilizing him, she owns him.

I've always been troubled by the picture de Brunhoff drew of that parting scene. Babar, Celeste, and Arthur, dressed to kill, drive off in Babar's automobile, while Celeste's and Arthur's mothers, naked as elephants, follow along behind the car with their trunks lifted up "to avoid breathing the dust." Babar, the male, drives, and the mothers, both uncivilized, trot along behind. The parents are made to follow their remade children while they are at the same time, losing them. Power has been transferred to the young Europeanized generation.

In de Brunhoff's illustrations the civilized elephants have personal identity and distinction; the natural elephants are portrayed as indistinguishable from each other. Here we see where the power is when the wild and the civilized make contact. Every time I looked at the book as a child, I felt there was something here that wasn't right. The mothers weren't being treated fairly. They should have been the ones in the car and the children should have been running behind, or they should all have been together in the car. Yet that wouldn't work either, since the idea of dressed and naked elephants riding together seemed embarrassing to me. That illustration was and is painful for me to look at.

The concept of nakedness is introduced here in a dramatic way. In the first page of the book, when we see Babar being rocked to sleep in a hammock by his mother, the elephants seem natural. Of course they have no clothes since elephants don't wear clothes. When Babar becomes dressed, there are no elephants around, so there is no thought of naked elephants. But as soon as the civilized Babar encounters naked elephants the question of deficiency arises. Babar is normal where he is living and the other elephants are deficient. Civilization creates desires which turn into necessities. If Celeste and Arthur are to associate with Babar, they must be dressed. Their mothers' natural state now becomes "nakedness" by contrast. Once Babar and his cousins reach home, the mother elephants merge into the crowd, indistinguishable from all the other elephants. We never see them again, and they cannot even be made out at Babar's marriage to Celeste; Celeste's mother is lost in the crowd of no-face elephants, her power completely obliterated.

Babar returns to his jungle home to find a crisis in the elephant patriarchy; the old king has died, and a new king is selected. The reader is presented with the dominance of males in the elephant world, and that's that.

The elephants see Babar, Arthur, and Celeste and exclaim, "What beautiful clothes! What a beautiful car!" and, at the suggestion of the oldest elephant, Cornelius, choose Babar as their new king since he has "learned so much living among men." All we are shown of his learning is that he knows how to choose clothes, order a meal at a restaurant, and add 2+2. He knows how to buy things and, once again, we see that power lies with money.

Before accepting his crown Babar (not Celeste) lets everyone know that he and Celeste have become engaged and they must accept Celeste as queen if they are to have him as king. There is no indication that Celeste has had much of a say in their engagement or anything else for that matter.

The elephants accept Babar's condition and shout in unison: "Long Live Queen Celeste! Long Live King Babar!"

After Babar's coronation King Babar praises the wise old Cornelius for having good ideas (the only one we hear about in the book is the idea that Babar should be king) and says, ". . . therefore I will make you general, and when I get my crown, I will give you my hat."—a touch of civilization for the general who is to rule when Babar and Celeste go on a honeymoon in a beautiful yellow balloon (another result of the Rich Lady's largesse, one has to presume). Thus power is given to the male military by the Europeanized king who goes off to new adventures.

What might children learn from this? I asked friends of mine who also read *Babar* as children if they remembered this scene, and without exception they did. In fact they remembered thinking it was a wonderful triumph for poor Babar who had lost his mother. One of these friends told me that she now hates the scene that shows Babar with his arm resting on Celeste's shoulder, Celeste with her head bowed, and the oldest elephant, Cornelius, with his glasses on, handing to Babar power over all the elephants. What had appeared magical to her as a child now represented the triumph of the Europeanized male. Did it harm her to have loved this scene as a child? Perhaps. It was one of many children's books that showed her that women's happiness derives from being chosen by the right male. Should she have been given a copy of *Babar* to read when she was six? Perhaps not.

She had this insight while reading the book to her oldest child in the early 1980s and vowed never to read it to any other child. It wasn't just *Babar* that she rejected but all children's books that presented women in subservient roles. She brought up the issue of having *Babar* and books like it in the library at the co-op nursery school that her children attended. This led the parents in the school to reread these books with a critical sensibility. Up to that time the parent group had simply accepted without comment the books they'd found in the library.

This critical reading came up with statistics that surprised the parents. Almost all the books were popular children's books found in most nurseries those days, though there were a few with an emphasis on cooperation instead of competition, and several on peace and racial harmony. Nevertheless, almost without exception, females were portrayed in the books as passive, dependent, and best when most domesticated. This was completely contrary to the values of most of the parents, so the questions arose: How much influence do these books have on children? Should they throw out all the old books that portrayed values contrary to theirs? And where were they to find new books with different values that were still as charming and compelling as much of traditional literature?

The parent group never reached a consensus. Some parents read books like *Babar* and discussed them with the children, others made up their own stories, and some had children make up stories and share them with the group. Friends of a few of the parents actually formed a number of small presses and published books of their own that were explicitly feminist and antiracist. The question of what to do with *Babar*, however, was never directly faced.

It is troubling for people who believe in a strong free press and want to trust their children's judgment to face the issue of censorship. Despite the desire to have their children exposed to the widest range of books, and especially the classics of children's literature, they also want their children to be free of sexist and racist attitudes. Yet in our society it is just about impossible to protect children from a barrage of sexist and racist books, videos, and comics aimed directly at them. The temptation to control children's reading and exposure to television and movies is not surprising, and for many parents it exists in uneasy tension with the desire to let children have free access to books and media.

SHOULD WE PROTECT OUR CHILDREN FROM *BABAR* AND BARBIE?

This raises the issue of how pure a book has to be for it to benefit children. Should there be no princes or kings, no princesses or queens, no portrayal of the benefits of wealth or the nature of male-centered families? Should children be protected from many of the classics of children's literature if these works seem to celebrate oppression, embody racism, or provide images of women as subordinate to men?

Two stories come to mind. A friend of mine who has two sons decided to prohibit them from playing with toy guns. One of the boys seemed to have a passion to play rough with guns. My perception of him was that he was gentle, not particularly violent or troubled. His friends had toy guns, and the fact that he was prohibited from having one made them very desirable. I expect he was nudged along by his friends, who might have humiliated him and accused him of letting his parents get away with too much. (Unfortunately, in our culture many middle-class kids become critical of their parents for depriving them of what they see as the necessary trappings of their class status. Certain toys become "necessities" for children bombarded by ads, comics, and TV.) In this case the boy, Steven, reached the limits of his frustration and screamed at his mother, "If you don't let me play with toy guns now, when I'm grown up I'm going to get real guns, and then you won't be able to stop me from using them."

Steven's mother was stunned, and we talked a lot about the situation. She decided not to respond to his threat immediately, but let him buy a toy pistol with money he had saved up a few weeks later. I remember he played with toy violence for a few weeks and then moved on to other things. Now he is a gourmet chef who looks back on the incident with amusement.

In a more personal case, my daughters passionately wanted Barbie dolls when they were six and seven. My wife and I had some serious doubts, and in my case, though I love and collect toys, I found Barbie and her entourage repugnant. We were both concerned about the effect Barbie would have on the girls' images of themselves as women if Barbie got too deep into their souls. However, their nagging and their argument that Barbie was just a toy and they knew the difference between dolls and people persuaded us to give in. I convinced myself that since I had overcome a heavy dose of World War II games of violence, casual and everyday sexism on the part of the older males in my home environment as a child, and a passion for reading boys' and girls' adventure books and fairy tales, my daughters could recover from Barbie. I believed this would be especially true if Barbie was used creatively and if Barbie was not their whole life.

I suggested that the girls make their own costumes for Barbie and use the dolls in games where Barbie and her friends did everything from building skyscrapers to flying planes. They did some of what I suggested and seemed to enjoy it, but sometimes they played with Barbies in ways that Barbie's manufacturer intended. Did it harm them? I asked my daughters, who are now in their mid-twenties and are both confirmed feminists. Their response was that playing with Barbies was fun, and Erica reminded me that she and Tonia always knew they were toys and not reality. She also reminded me that they loved Barbie's Dune Buggy and used to build sand cities and develop complex scenarios for their fantasy adventures, which also included stuffed animals, some of my toys and figurines, and other artistic creations of their own. They had felt free to play the Barbie script or change it; once they even had a long game that they called S&M Barbie, in which they tied up Barbie and Ken.

One of their friends, who is African American, also had a Barbie collection. She, as well as my daughters, had African American Barbies as well as White ones, and they played out all the ranges and varieties of sexual unions possible with the palette at their command. Interracial love, gay and lesbian love, the love of people dolls for stuffed animals, all figured in their fantasy play.

Both Tonia and Erica pointed out that they knew Barbie's body was silly and perverse, that Barbie was nothing like their mom, Judy, and that the thought of my being like Ken was absolutely hilarious. However, they did say that they have met young women in their lives for whom Barbie was a more serious matter. It is Erica's analysis that the damaging effects of Barbie arise with children whose fathers act as if women were dolls and whose mothers buy into the idea that Barbie-like styling is "the" model of beauty. In these cases the problem is more complex than the toys children use, and the Barbies are part of a complex that can lead to bulimia and anorexia at worst, or to other problems with one's body and sexuality. For Erica the problem is the context in which Barbie is set rather than Barbie itself.

Besides, Tonia pointed out, there was no avoiding knowing about Barbies and there was no avoiding the danger they held of socializing young girls to become sex objects. If you were prevented from playing with them, they became more attractive. I know several people in their twenties who collect old Barbies with a vengeance, having been prohibited from playing with them as children. However, this doesn't seem to interfere with their commitment to feminism or their rejection of the oppression of women. It is a benign contradiction in their lives of the sort people have when they grow up at cross-purposes to the society they live in.

More generally, there is no way to avoid having your children exposed to many objectionable or problematic aspects of our culture. Guns and Barbies, and *Babar* too, are part of cultural life in the United States, and children have to develop critical attitudes toward them. These attitudes will not develop through prohibition. On the contrary, what will more likely develop is a distaste for parental authority and a heightened critical scrutiny of adult life. The challenge parents face is how to integrate encounters with stereotypes into their children's sensibility and help their children become critical of aspects of the culture that denigrate or humiliate them or anyone else. The challenge is also how to let children feel free to develop their own evaluation of cultural practices. Instead of prohibiting things that tempt children, this means allowing them the freedom to explore things while trusting them to make sensible and humane judgments. It also means being explicitly critical of books and TV and encouraging children to discuss questions of judgment and values. This might seem a bit abstract, but I have found that watching TV and questioning what one sees, that visiting a toy store and suggesting which behaviors certain dolls and toys are designed to influence, can begin as early as children can talk. Nor need it be a grim exercise.

One of the places where I drew a hard line with my children was with G.I. Joe war toys, which socialize all children to accept war as play. I tried as much as possible to explain to my children how they represented the worst in people, glorified killing, and made war seem a casual matter of play. I even refused to buy them for my children, though I didn't prohibit them from using allowances or birthday or Christmas money to buy them. At the time, our three children (Josh the youngest as well as his two sisters) were exposed to G.I. Joe, my wife and I were actively engaged in protesting the Vietnam War. We took the children on marches when it was safe, explained to them what we were protesting, why we were doing it, and what risks we decided to take. The whole experience of the antiwar movement must have had a profound influence on them, for there was never any question of their buying the dolls or playing with them with friends. My son, Josh, became a pacifist at a very early age and still is one, and my daughters are profoundly antiwar. I suppose if they had bought G.I. Joe and played at making war I would have found a way to tolerate it, but I am sure it would have upset me deeply. Still, I don't believe it would have been my business to do more than try to influence them with reason and with the force of my example in the adult world.

Children will not come to a healthy critical stance without adult help. It is not developmentally inevitable that children will learn how to evaluate with sensitivity and intelligence what the adult world presents them. It is our responsibility, as critical and sensitive adults, to nurture the development of this sensibility in our children. This may require letting them play with Barbies, putting our foot down when it comes to G.I. Joe, and still keeping the door open for them to disagree with us without our rejecting them. In my experience, children quickly come to understand that critical sensibility strengthens them. It allows them to stand their ground, to develop opinions that are consistent with deeply held values, and, when conscience requires it, to act against consensus or the crowd. It is a source of pleasure as well—of the joy that comes from feeling that one is living according to conviction and understanding rather than being subject to the pressures and seductions of others.

Babar, my token for what is objectionable in children's literature, is a cultural phenomenon, an established children's classic that most children are likely to encounter. Often the question is not *whether* they encounter Babar, but *how*. Are they aware of colonialism? Do they understand that civilizing the elephants is symbolic of destroying the culture of colonized people? Or that the beneficent free-flowing money of the Rich Lady is a form of glorifying the ruling class? And does it matter? At this point I can imagine a reader wondering whether all this analysis is more than a book like *Babar* merits, but more people in the United States have probably read *Babar* than have read most best-sellers and classics. They buy the book for their children and read it together, and that's reason enough to take the text seriously; it becomes part of people's cultural heritage or cultural baggage, depending upon how you look at it. And we all have an abiding soft spot for *Babar*. We put aside the colonialism, the implied racism and sexism of the tale that are apparent upon rereading it. The image of the poor young elephant who has no father and whose mother is killed is powerful. What else could he do but fall into any temptation, and who among us could say they would resist the Rich Lady?

Recently I heard a speech given by Laurent de Brunhoff, the son of Jean de Brunhoff, the creator of Babar. The son is writing new sequels to *Babar* (there are many old sequels written by Jean de Brunhoff himself). Laurent said explicitly that he's trying to update Babar's image and indicated that he was very aware of the power relationships represented in the book and the way in which they imply support of sexism, racism, and colonialism. Thus, the analysis here is not unique. Analysis of the content of *Babar* and many other children's books is fairly common practice in commercial publishing houses, particularly those that sell to a school market increasingly sensitive about stereotyping. The publishers show little reluctance to censor or change original texts, so it is important to develop textual analysis of one's own and examine whether publishers, in the name of cleaning up old textbooks, aren't in fact introducing other equally distressing biases. For example, in an article published in the Teachers and Writers Collaborative Newsletter in the fall of 1989, Nancy Kricorian described a twelve-page editor's taboo list she was given by a textbook publisher that hired her to find poems for a reading series they were developing. She says the list "forbade the mention of ghosts, magic, religion, tobacco, cheating, sugar and candy. Birthday cake, death, divorce, negative emotions, and religious holidays were to be avoided." In their attempt to root out every possible bias and please everybody, the publishers extinguished life in all its complexity and variability, and in doing so routed much of good poetry from the series. The hunt for hidden bias should not create an image of life that corresponds to no lived experience. Racism, sexism, and colonialism, as well as suicide, divorce, and cheating, figure in life and literature, and should certainly be read about and discussed at home and in the classroom. It's when books explicitly propagandize for inequality and misery that one has to be careful about how and whether they are used with young children who are not explicitly aware of their biases.

IS *BABAR* PROPAGANDA?

Does *Babar* explicitly propagandize children through the way power works in the story? So far I have discussed several questions about the nature of power in *Babar*. Some other questions are, Who wants power, and Who takes others' power from them? Are there any power struggles in the book? And if so, how are they dealt with?

Babar doesn't covet power. In fact, he seems to throw it away or at least delegate it to old Cornelius so he and Celeste can go on adventures. The Rich Lady provides a model of life without working, and Babar embraces it. Not for him the weight of kingship. He heads off in his balloon and ventures among the world of people. The military establishment will take care of things.

There are no apparent power struggles in the book, but let's imagine what might happen when Babar and Celeste leave the jungle. What we have left behind is Cornelius, the general, who wears Babar's hat, and cousin Arthur, who is dressed in people clothes. All the other elephants are naked, including Arthur's own mother. Do we have an incipient class structure developing? Will Arthur join with Cornelius, or will he try to displace him? Will other elephants join with Arthur, or develop their own type of clothes made from indigenous materials and raise a rebellion for local control and against the foreign influences Babar imported to the jungle? Will there be a purist rebellion of elephants who believe that it is in the nature of elephanthood to be naked and will try to purge all signs of foreign influence? Will the female elephants claim power? And will they be purists, local developers, or imitators? Or will the military mobilize itself and establish and maintain order in the name of the absent king? Or maybe even throw off monarchy and develop an elephant oligarchy or military dictatorship? One thing is for sure; things will never be the same after Babar's return.

In *Babar* the symbols, signs, and rituals of power and of loyalty work throughout the story and become unspoken ways of getting children to acknowledge the validity of the power relations portrayed. Babar's power, for example, is represented by his clothes, his hat, and his car. The two naked mother elephants stand out in the city. Their nakedness is not a sign merely of their innocence but of their naiveté, their ignorance, and their vulnerability (to the hunter as well as the city). A dressed and educated elephant is something else, the kind of creature who can stand by the fireplace, recounting wild tales to amuse the civilized. Babar's standing in front of the fireplace, telling the Rich Lady's friends tales of the jungle, reminds me of another children's story about Pocahontas, the Native American woman who saved John Smith in the Virginia colony and was taken back to England by him. The story tells how she amused the people in the court of King James in London, where she lived the rest of her life. According to the myth constructed by European American authors, she told tales of her own people, about their quaint habits and culture. One wonders what she thought of these strangers, and whether it occurred to her that they considered her people savages and her tales justification for considering Native Peoples less than fully human. Or, more likely, was the story of the benign and friendly Pocahontas a tale invented to soothe the consciences of White people whose ancestors had practiced genocide?

Many of the rituals of power in *Babar* reinforce some of the least functional habits in our society. The first ritual, one that might certainly interest many children in our society, is going shopping. Not only does Babar shop; he can get anything he wants. What a dream for young children whose lives are full of "I want" and "buy me." This ritual makes Babar similar to, but luckier than, most children, and may account for much of the book's popularity in the capitalist world. I know I often imagined as a kid what it would be like to be able to get anything I wanted, and my cousin Marlyn and friends Bobby and Ronny used to make up imaginary shopping lists and compare them. Wanting things is serious business in our society, and I feel uncomfortable with books that reinforce that obsession.

Marriage is another ritual, and Babar's marriage is an interesting one. He marries his cousin, Celeste, perhaps keeping the royal line within the family. Cousin marriages are not well regarded in our society, and teachers I've spoken with get very nervous about this aspect of the Babar story. They try to skip over it in class, redirect discussion, or tie the issue up by saying that elephants have a different sense of family than people do. However the relationship between Celeste and Babar is not based on their mutual elephantness at all. It's based on his being able to dress and thereby civilize her. Their mutual distance from the community of their origin is a defining part of their relationship, a fact that might cause some people in immigrant communities in the United States some pause.

There is another place in *Babar* where the maintenance of power raises some interesting questions. Babar gives his derby hat to Cornelius as a symbol of the transference of power. Yet how is a hat enough to ensure that Cornelius can maintain authority over the other elephants? This raises the question of the power of symbols and the role of vested authority in children's literature. I am convinced that children believe in the power of objects such as scepters, wands, and crowns, all of which have a symbolic relation to authority. These objects, when used in tales and stories, reinforce ideas of how authority is legitimized and transferred. Babar becomes king because he is better than the other elephants, and his power is transferred through his hat to Cornelius, who is thereby deemed qualified to rule. Therefore Cornelius becomes qualified to rule. That's not dissimilar to a teacher making a child a monitor in a classroom and giving her or him a badge or a pencil and pad to write down the names of miscreants regardless of whether the role is a suitable one for the child or whether the other children will recognize that authority.

The use of symbols and possessions to legitimize authority is dangerous and antidemocratic. It suggests to children that blind acceptance of authority is good behavior. The question of whether one encourages a child to accept or question authority is a major one in childrearing. It is generally assumed that children should not question adult authority. Yet, in a world where there is so much illegitimate authority, or legitimized authority that acts in illegitimate ways, knowing how to question authority is very healthy. Books that slip in, as a characteristic of reality, the acceptance and transference of kingly authority give little credit to democratic citizenship and could conceivably set up young people for obediently fighting in other people's wars and believing that their vote and voice does not count for much in the world. One compelling reason for not reading *Babar* is that it makes a thoroughly undemocratic way of governance seem natural and unquestioned.

The establishment and maintenance of power is presented as a major theme at the very beginning of the story. The hunter kills Babar's mother. He who owns the gun has the power over life and death. Babar knows this, and when he stumbles into a human world and gets seduced into adopting its ways, does he forget his mother's killer? Or does he always keep, somewhere in the recesses of his mind, the fact that if he crosses the Rich Lady or does something really wrong in the world of people his mother's fate awaits him? This reading makes *Babar* a much sadder story than it is usually taken to be, one colored at every point by guns, death, and the cruelty of people. Babar in this reading is a frightened, obedient slave who is allowed to go home, but not without wearing the mark of oppression.

I have recently discovered that pointing this out to children can have a devastating effect on their reaction to the story. I visited a third-grade class and gave them a talk on the making of this essay. I told them that my motivation was to examine the different meanings that could be found in *Babar*. Then I defined colonialism and pointed out that the costume of the hunter gave him away as a colonist. Next I gave them some history of French colonialism in Africa, and we discussed the meaning of clothes in the story. There is no reason why a discussion like this shouldn't be part of the critical literature program as early as the third grade, if not earlier. Not surprisingly, one of the questions that arose in our discussion was what Babar felt about the death of his mother. Why didn't he stomp on some of the people he encountered? And why did the author never mention anything about bringing the hunter to justice? Finally the issue of what Babar learned from people came up, and to the group it seemed that he no longer liked being an elephant. Thus, not only was he not trying to avenge the death of his mother; in a way he became the friend of his mother's murderers. Frantz Fanon described this internalization of the colonists' culture as one of the deepest forms of dehumanization experienced by the victims of colonialism, one which, according to him, can only be overcome through bloody revolution. The third-graders must have sensed some of this, because most of them expressed anger at the hunter and no longer thought the story was cute or charming.

Do children who have not had an opportunity to analyze the text see this sinister aspect of the Babar story? Most youngsters I've questioned seem to acknowledge its existence and then forget it. They just want that man with the gun out of the story, never to come back and haunt Babar's life. However, one summer, during the year I was teaching at a school for severely disturbed children, I lived with a seven-year-old boy who had been classified as childhood schizophrenic. Mark was a brilliant reader and often memorized books that he'd read. At night, when he was alone in his bedroom, I could hear him talking to characters in his favorite books. *Babar* was one of them. Mark was obsessed with the death scene at the beginning of the book and had made up a name for the hunter, creating a whole scenario for the hunt, which ended in Babar's mother's death. For him, death hung over the book. He wondered whether the clerks in the store knew the hunter, speculated that one of the Rich Lady's friends was the hunter, and told Babar over and over again in imaginary conversation that he would be killed just like his mother was killed, even by the same hunter.

Mark's case was extreme, but the murder at the beginning of the story is remembered by everyone who reads the book. It is what bonds the reader to Babar and makes one want him to be treated well. Yet the death is awful and arbitrary, and reminds one of the importance of current attempts to ban the sale of ivory and eliminate elephant poaching. So, is it good or bad that children read about the cold-blooded murder of a mother in front of her child, even if they are elephants in a fantasy tale? Especially when there is no revenge or justice in the story? What if some children identify with the hunter and not Babar or his mother? Is that reason enough to ban or burn the book? Or can children bear the unpleasant along with the pleasant, and do they even need it as a way to help them face the fact that life ends in death?

These seem like profound and complex questions to raise in the context of thinking about a short children's classic. Yet critical reading consists of questioning a text, challenging it, and speculating on ways in which the world it creates can illuminate the one we live in. A book is a wonderful tutor for the imagination which thrives on being challenging as much as it does on being challenged. Part of the experience of reading *Babar* for a child is raising questions, like Did Babar forget his mother when he met the Rich Lady? Did he ever talk to her about his mother? What happened between Celeste and Arthur in that car ride back to the jungle that led to getting married? Why is wearing clothes so important in this story? And what would I do if I met the Rich Lady?

For a more experienced and older reader, the challenges can go beyond the text itself to inquiries about the author's politics, social class, and family background, and to speculation about the emotional impact of books in general that show children losing their parents. In all of these cases, reading becomes dialogue. The text can be reimagined and invested with multiple meanings. For the active reader, there is no need for one authoritative interpretation, and even absurd fights over the meaning of the text are part of the whole experience of reading. However, read uncritically, there is always the possibility that a book like *Babar* can contribute to the formation of stereotypes and attitudes that might be reinforced by other reading, by TV, and by the nature and shape of the toys manufactured for children's use. Children's books contribute to the formation of culture, and some books can even transform the way children look at and relate to the world. Therefore the question of reading Babar, for me, can be reduced to the question of whether uncritical reading of the book is so potentially damaging that it should be withheld from children when possible.

There is even more to the case of *Babar*. Thinking about the death of Babar's mother leads to another question related to power: How does a story define and deal with good and evil? In *Babar* the hunter is evil, but if there is any other evil present it is hidden from obvious view. The elephants are simple and good. In fact they trust and admire people so much that they're willing to give up their elephant nature for some clothes and a car. The Rich Lady, who is "very rich," is also portrayed as good and generous. And Babar, when all dressed up, is also good. It's important to note that he is not dressed like a taxicab driver in Paris or a salesman or factory worker; he's dressed like an entrepreneur with a little derby hat and spats on his shoes. These are symbols of the upper class, but in this book they are also symbols of goodness. The rich are good, money is good, simple elephants who believe those things are also good. Babar's mother is good, but isn't the hunter who "is wicked" also dressed in a way that identifies him as upper class? Could there be a relationship between hunting and money? Is the hunter's evil also to be found in the city? We are never told. The story sweeps evil under the rug. The hunter disappears. With him also goes what might have created wrenching tension in the story. I can, however, imagine an adult version of *Babar* that centers around Babar, dressed to kill, hunting down the killer of his mother, and killing him in an elephant way in the midst of his family somewhere in Paris. However, *Babar* isn't an adult thriller or a psychological novel about revenge and the myths of primitivity and civilization. It's a story for little children, and its main tension comes from Babar's loneliness for his elephant friends and his life in the jungle.

Studying how tension and dissonance are dealt with in a plot is another way of discovering the role of power relations in a story. Babar is drawn home and has to leave the Rich Lady. However, she has made a lasting change in his life, one that affects the way he returns home and his subsequent need to leave and travel in the world outside the jungle. In the gentlest and most seductive way, Babar has given up his elephant power and become a bit of a dandy. One way of reading this central theme in the story is that Babar has been marginalized in both the human and animal worlds by his contact with the Rich Lady. The ruling class has made him dependent on money and things without giving him any independent way to earn them. It has also taken away his identity as an elephant among elephants. He is an exile, a stranger in a strange land and in his own land at the same time.

A less political reader might find all of this farfetched. She or he might see the book as a way of getting children to overcome fear of large wild animals. Of course this is just speculation, playing around with reading. Children most likely see Babar as a kid elephant with all four feet in two worlds simultaneously. And they see him as part of a story, one take on many imaginary worlds, not as a character in a cautionary tale about identity. It's easy to take children's literature more seriously than children take it, and it's sensible, in the midst of critical musings, to remember that sometimes an elephant in a green suit is just an elephant in a green suit.

WHAT'S MISSING FROM *BABAR*?

So far I've been looking at power relationships within the text of *Babar*. Another way to examine the book is to step outside of it and consider what is not in the text. This is a bit like trying to understand the nature of a private political meeting from a list of people who weren't invited. Who has been uninvited to Babar's world? Among others, working-class people who don't work in stores and serve the rich; poor people; human children; and humans Babar's age. The people in Paris don't all live like the Rich Lady, her friends, and the people that serve them. Providing young children with a steady diet of the untroubled lives of the rich (there is no friction in the Rich Lady's world and no apparent pain) is one way to equate wealth with well-being. Though most books for young children don't portray a world of the rich and their servants, and are much more middle class in character, they still tie well-being to money and portray lives full of comfort and joy. By implication they provide an ideal type of life, one worth aspiring to. However, it is possible to live a full and decent life without great wealth, and it may be that the acquisition of great wealth always comes at the cost of other peoples' impoverishment. These possibilities are rarely if ever raised in children's literature.

I mentioned this once to a group of parents who are friends of ours, mostly middle-class academics, whose response in part was: Why not let children remain innocent for a while and be given stories about people who live well and enjoy life? My response is that there are many ways to live well, and it's important to show children that you don't have to be rich to live well, that living well is not simply a matter of being able to buy things and have other people take care of your everyday needs. Of course, there's probably nothing wrong with allowing an occasional elephant with a green jacket who can buy everything he wants into children's lives if there are other visions for them to ponder as well.

There is another major absence in the tale of Babar, one that I remember worrying about. Where is Babar's father? There is no mention that Babar has a father in the entire story. Was his father also killed by a hunter? Did he leave home and abandon Babar and his mother? Did de Brunhoff consciously leave him out or simply forget to put him in? Or did he intend Babar to be born, like Jesus, without a father? Was Babar illegitimate or was he meant to be symbolically special so that when his mother is killed he becomes orphaned and can't be claimed by any family in the society? Is that a presage of his coming coronation and special relationship with the world of civilization? Or, to negate all of my idle chatter, my wife suggested that there was a much simpler interpretation. Elephants are polygamous, with the major males the only ones mating with all of the bearing female elephants. The analogy between the human nuclear family and the elephant herd completely breaks down here. In addition, polygamy was illegal and considered sinful in de Brunhoff's world. Perhaps, rather than bring up the issue of anthropomorphism, he simply skirted the question of Babar's paternity.

These days publishers of children's books resist stories that personalize animals because the analogy between human and animal life is never exact. There is more concern than in the past about providing accurate descriptions of animal life. It's possible that if de Brunhoff were to submit *Babar* for publication these days it would be rejected for scientific inaccuracy as well as for its portrayal of colonialism and gender, and its implications of racism. Yet this too is an interesting issue with respect to children's book classics: How many of them would be accepted for publication today given the current increased sensitivity to issues of gender, race, and homophobia?

SHOULD WE BURN *BABAR*?

So, finally, what are we to do with this charming elephant in a green suit who, despite all of these complaints, attracts and amuses many children? What are we to do about the "universal" experiences of fun and fantasy the book can provide to all children? Are we to deprive children of them? Or do they even exist?

Universal is a big word. Is it true that children in South Africa or any of the former French colonies in Africa will find *Babar* amusing? Do young children there need to read such a remnant of colonialism? Don't they have other things to be concerned with and other delightful stories and tales to be regaled with? I would find it sensible in that context to consign *Babar* to the children's literature research library or use it as a text to be studied in a class on the instruments of colonialism, or on critical thinking and the development of child intelligence.

I recently faced a situation similar to this one. During the quincentenary celebration of Columbus's invasion of the Americas I received over a dozen children's books on Columbus for review. While cleaning out my library I came upon the books and had to decide what to do with them.

Usually I loan review copies of books to teachers at our local schools or give them to the town library. However, I found all of these books objectionable, glorifying Columbus as they did. In most cases Native Peoples were either totally absent or represented as grateful for the arrival of civilization. It was astonishing to me, given the amount of attention supposedly paid to the sensitivities of Native Americans in current publishing, how like the old books even the newest and most elegant Columbus books were. I read some of them with parents of a few of the Native American youngsters I worked with, and they were offended and wouldn't show them to their young children, who already knew enough about being stereotyped by White culture. So, should I burn these books? There seemed few other options. I refused to donate them to the library or the school since I agreed that children needed a truthful and compassionate view of the European colonization of the Americas. My decision was to save two of the books for our library as examples to critique and to take the rest to the dump and bury them. It was hard for me to make this decision as I love books and have no fear myself of reading anything. But in our school most of the teachers are not sensitive to the insults these books contain, and I didn't want to contribute to this insensitivity.

This has to do with the question of what children learn from "good" literature written for their consumption. This last question assumes that all children have some common traits that lie at the core of their appreciation of "good" literature. However, using the word "children" masks the differences in experience and culture that shapes appreciation and pleasure. It opens up seemingly logical and coherent arguments to bias and misunderstanding. I remember talking about *Babar* with a friend of mine who is a Black South African from Capetown. I showed him the book, and he stopped at the second page, the one where the hunter is shooting Babar's mother. He told me that if children in his community saw that hunter, dressed in safari clothes with his white pith helmet, their response would not be sympathy with Babar and sadness over the death of his mother so much as hatred of the colonial with a gun. There are innumerable fables and stories in southern Africa that educate young Black children about the dangers of the White oppressors, some funny and some grim. Many have explicitly to do with a man dressed just as the hunter in *Babar* who tries to kill monkeys, elephants, or some other animals. According to my friend, who had been a school teacher before being sent into exile for his political activity, the fact that the hunter disappears after killing Babar's mother would puzzle and anger children he taught. To them, the hunter would be the antagonist in the story. Dressing up an elephant in a suit and putting a happy face on the story was an insult to them, and he couldn't imagine them finding anything amusing or edifying or charming about the whole thing.

In addition, he said that the analogy between the naked elephants and African people was so transparent and insulting as to make the book overtly racist and without redeeming factors from his perspective.

On the other hand, I remember my own children liking the books, mostly the drawings, which are charming. My wife, Judy, and I got the books for the children because we remembered loving them as children. Judy and I were not damaged for life by liking the books, but I do believe that they contributed to my not questioning many aspects of patriarchy earlier in life, and to a misunderstanding of the intensity of the horrors of colonialist attitudes. How much they contributed is hard to say. It's very difficult to sort out childhood influences and specify exactly how much one particular experience related to all of the other influences in one's environment.

I am pretty sure that my children would think carefully about whether to buy *Babar* for their own (not yet born) children. They are much more aware of stereotyping and bias in children's books than I was in my early twenties, and much more concerned about their damaging effect. In addition, there is a whole new literature for children that has emerged over the past twenty-five years, one that is built upon a sensitivity to bias and a vision of equality that was thoroughly absent in almost all the books written for children in the past. It is to this literature, I am confident, that they will turn to provide growing-up stories for their children. Certainly it is what I will draw upon if and when I become a grandparent.

I wouldn't ban or burn *Babar*, or pull it from libraries. But buy it? No. I see no reason to go out of one's way to make *Babar* available to children, primarily because I don't see much critical reading going on in the schools, and children don't need to be propagandized about colonialism, sexism, or racism. There are many other cute and well-illustrated, less offensive animal tales for young people. I believe *Babar* would best be relegated to the role of collector's item, an item in a museum of stereotypes. My wife disagrees. She has much more confidence than I do in children's ability to develop critical sensitivity unaided; she might buy it for our grandchildren after all.

Beyond her disagreement, there still is something else that makes me uncomfortable about my own conclusions. *Babar* has some appealing aspects. De Brunhoff's drawings and the story of his elephant in a green suit who has all the money and resources to do anything he cares to do can be looked at as a parable of freedom. The free unencumbered adventurer has its appeal, and I might dig out my old copy and share it with my grandchildren as an example of what us older people were reading almost fifty years ago. We'd discuss the limitations of de Brunhoff's vision, and maybe even reconceive the story as it might be told if it assumed a more equitable world as background for the action. I might do the same thing in my teaching. But, in both cases, I'd use *Babar* only if the children had been surrounded by a wealth of books and stories and tales, and had the opportunity to talk about the relationships of stories to people's dreams.

If there were only a few books a child had access to, it would be foolish to select any that have racial, class, or sexual bias woven into their content and imagery as positive things, no matter how charming or "classic" they are. *Babar*'s time as a central experience in childhood must pass. In this case I use the word "childhood" as a universally applicable noun.

THE STORY OF ROSA PARKS AND THE MONTGOMERY BUS BOYCOTT REVISITED

Racism, and the direct confrontation between African American and European American people in the United States, is an issue that is usually considered too sensitive to be dealt with directly in the elementary school classroom. When confrontation between African Americans and European Americans occurs in children's literature, it is routinely described as a problem between individuals that can be worked out on a personal basis. In the few cases where racism is addressed as a social problem, there has to be a happy ending. This is most readily apparent in the biographical treatment of Rosa Parks, one of the two names that most children in the United States associate with the Civil Rights movement in the southern United States during the 1960s; the other is Martin Luther King Jr.

Over the past few years, during visits to schools, I've talked with children about the Civil Rights movement. One of the things I ask the children is what they know of Rosa Parks and her involvement in the Montgomery bus boycott. This focus developed after I observed a play about civil rights in a fourth-grade classroom in southern California several years ago. One scene in the play took place on a bus in Montgomery, Alabama. A tired Rosa Parks got on the bus and sat down. The child portraying Mrs. Parks was dressed in shabby clothes and carried two worn shopping bags. She sat down next to the driver, and other children got on the bus until all the seats in front were filled up. Then a boy got on and asked her to move. She refused, and the bus driver told her he didn't want any trouble. Politely he asked her to move to the back of the bus. She refused again and the scene ended. In the next scene we see a crowd of students, African American and European American, carrying signs saying Don't Ride the Buses, We shall Overcome, and Blacks and Whites Together. One of the students, playing Martin Luther King Jr., addressed the rest of the class, saying something to the effect that African American and European American people in Montgomery got angry because Rosa Parks was arrested for not moving to the back of the bus, and that they were boycotting the buses until all people could ride wherever they wanted. The play ended with a narrator pointing out that the bus problem in Montgomery was solved by people coming together to protest peacefully for justice.

Before talking to the children about their perceptions of Rosa Parks and her motivations, I had a moment to talk with the teacher about a major misrepresentation of facts in the play: there were no European Americans involved in boycotting the buses in Montgomery. The struggle was organized and maintained by the African American community, and to represent it as an interracial struggle was to take the power and credit away from that community. The teacher agreed that the play took some liberty with history but said that since his class was interracial, it was better for all the children to do the play as an integrated struggle. Otherwise, he said, the play might lead to racial strife in the classroom. I disagreed and pointed out that by showing the power of organized African Americans, it might lead all the children to recognize and appreciate the strength oppressed people can show when confronting their oppressors. In addition, the fact that European Americans joined the struggle later on could lead to very interesting discussions about social change and struggles for justice, and could be related to the current situation in South Africa and the resurgence of overt racism in the United States. He disagreed and ended our chat by telling me how hard it was to manage an integrated classroom.

I contented myself with asking the children about Rosa Parks. The girl who played Mrs. Parks, Anna, told me that she imagined "Rosa," as she called Mrs. Parks, to be a poor woman who did tiring and unpleasant work. She added that she imagined Rosa was on her way home to a large family that she had to take care of all by herself when she refused to move to the back of the bus. In other words, Rosa Parks was, in her mind, a poor, single parent with lots of children, and an unskilled worker. I asked her how she got that idea, and she replied that's just the kind of person she felt Rosa Parks must be. She added that nobody had ever told her that her view was wrong, so she never bothered to question it. Her teacher backed her up and claimed that she had made reasonable assumptions about Rosa Parks, ones that he felt were true to the way Rosa Parks was portrayed in the books they had in class. I couldn't argue with that last comment.

I changed the subject and asked Anna why Rosa Parks's arrest led to a boycott. She said she didn't know. Maybe Rosa had a friend who told everybody, or maybe it was in the newspaper. One of the other students suggested that her arrest was on TV and everybody came out to protest because they didn't think it was right to arrest someone just for not moving to the back of the bus. The boycott was, to them, some form of spontaneous action that involved no planning or strategy.

All the children admired Rosa Parks for not moving. Some said she must be a very stubborn person, others that she had to be so angry that she didn't care what happened to her. They agreed that it took a special person to be so courageous and wondered if they would be able to muster such courage. I got the impression that Mrs. Parks's exceptional courage might be an excuse for them to not act.

I decided to push the issue a bit and asked the class why Rosa Parks had to move to the back of the bus anyway. One of the African American children said it was segregated in the South back then, and African Americans and European Americans couldn't do things together. When I asked why there was segregation in those days there was absolute silence. I shifted a bit and asked if the African Americans and European Americans in their classroom could do things together. One of the boys answered, "In school they do, mostly." Since I was just a guest I left it at that. However, it was clear to me that issues of racial conflict were not explicitly discussed in this classroom, and that the play about the Montgomery bus boycott left the children with some vague sense of unity and victory, but with no sense of the risk and courage of the African American people who originated the struggle for civil rights in the United States or of the history and nature of segregation. I have no idea whether there was any racism manifest in the everyday lives of the children in that classroom, but wondered whether they or the teacher were at all prepared to deal with it if it erupted.

The children's visualization of Rosa Parks, whom they felt free to call by her first name, was particularly distressing. As well as poor, they imagined her to be without education or sophistication, a person who acted on impulse and emotion rather than intelligence and moral conviction. There was no sense of her as a community leader or as part of an organized struggle against oppression. I decided to find out how common this view was, and I have been astonished to find that those children's view of Rosa

Parks is not at all different from that of most European American adults and almost all the school children I have questioned.

The image of "Rosa the Tired," and the story that goes with it, exists on the level of a national cultural icon in the United States. School textbooks and children's books are major perpetuators of this myth, but none of them I've seen quote sources for their distorted personal information about Mrs. Parks. Yet, most American children's first encounter with the Civil Rights movement comes through these writings. Dozens of children's books and textbooks I've looked at present the same version of Rosa Parks and the Montgomery bus boycott. This version can be reduced to the following generic story, which I fabricated* and could be titled:

"ROSA WAS TIRED: THE STORY OF THE MONTGOMERY BUS BOYCOTT"

Rosa Parks was a poor seamstress. She lived in Montgomery, Alabama, during the 1950s. In those days there was still segregation in parts of the United States. That meant that African Americans and European Americans were not allowed to use the same public facilities such as restaurants or swimming pools. It also meant that whenever it was crowded on the city buses African Americans had to give up seats in front to European Americans and move to the back of the bus.

One day on her way home from work Rosa was tired and sat down in the front of the bus. As the bus got crowded she was asked to give up her seat to a European American man, and she refused. The bus driver told her she had to go to the back of the bus, and she still refused to move. It was a hot day, and she was tired and angry, and became very stubborn.

The driver called a policeman, who arrested Rosa.

When other African Americans in Montgomery heard this they became angry too, so they decided to refuse to ride the buses until everyone was allowed to ride together. They boycotted the buses.

The boycott, which was led by Martin Luther King Jr., succeeded. Now African Americans and European Americans can ride the buses together in Montgomery.

Rosa Parks was a very brave person.

*See the note on references at the end of this article for the specific sources I drew upon to create this generic version of Rosa Parks's story.

This story seems innocent enough. Rosa Parks is treated with respect and dignity and the African American community is given credit for running the boycott and winning the struggle. It reflects the view of Mrs. Parks often found in adult literature as well as writings for children. For example, in the book by eminent psychiatrist Robert Coles, *The Moral Life of Children* (Boston: Houghton Mifflin, 1986), we find the following quote:

> We had come to know . . . a group of poor and poorly educated people, who, nevertheless, acquitted themselves impressively in pursuit of significant ethical objectives. I think of Rosa Parks, a seamstress, whose decision to sit where she pleased on a Montgomery, Alabama, bus in the middle 1950s preceded the emergence of the so-called Civil Rights movement and of Dr. King and Ralph Abernathy as leaders of it. (p. 25)

A more recent example of this can be found in Robert Fulghum's best-selling book, *It Was on Fire When I Lay Down on It.* (Ivy Books, 1988)

> I write this on the first day of December in 1988, the anniversary of a moment when someone sat still and lit the fuse to social dynamite. On this day in 1955, a forty-two-year-old woman was on her way home from work. Getting on a public bus, she paid her fare and sat down on the first vacant seat. It was good to sit down—her feet were tired. As the bus filled with passengers, the driver turned and told her to give up her seat and move on back in the bus. She sat still. The driver got up and shouted, "MOVE IT!" She sat still. Passengers grumbled, cursed her, pushed at her. Still she sat. So the driver got off the bus, called the police, and they came to haul her off to jail and into history.
>
> Rosa Parks. Not an activist or a radical. Just a quiet, conservative, churchgoing woman with a nice family and a decent job as a seamstress. For all the eloquent phrases that have been turned about her place in the flow of history, she did not get on that bus looking for trouble or trying to make a statement. Going home was all she had in mind, like everybody else. She was anchored to her seat by her own dignity. Rosa Parks simply wasn't going to be a "nigger" for anybody anymore. And all she knew to do was to sit still. (pp. 109-10)

And here's a current textbook version of the Montgomery bus boycott story written for elementary school children. It comes from the Heath

Social Studies series for elementary school, *Exploring My World* by Jeff Passe and Evangeline Nicholas (Lexington, MA: 1991, D.C. Heath, reproduced on page 188 of the Teachers' Guide) and is similar in content to my generic tale:

> When Rosa Parks rode on a bus, she had to sit all the way in the back. Her city had a law. It said black people could not sit in the front of a bus.
>
> One day Rosa was tired. She sat inthe front. The bus driver told her to move. She did not. He called the police. Rosa was put in jail.
>
> Some citizens tried to help. One of them was Martin Luther King Jr. The citizens decided to stop riding buses until the law was changed.
>
> Their plan worked. The law was changed. Soon, many other unfair laws were changed. Rosa Parks led the way!

The Teachers' Guide to this text informs teachers that "Mrs. Parks' single act brought about the desegregation of buses all over the country." In a lesson plan referring to Rosa Parks's being told to move to the back of the bus, it informs teachers to "tell children they will be reading about a woman who became angry when this happened to her. She decided she was not being treated fairly, and she was not going to put up with that kind of treatment anymore. Have children read to find out how the actions of Rosa Parks helped to change the way black people were treated." (p. 188)

This book was published in 1991 and is certainly still in use. It encourages presenting the Montgomery bus boycott as the single act of a person who was tired and angry. Intelligent and passionate opposition to racism is simply not part of the story. In the entire part of the guide dealing with the Montgomery bus boycott, there is no mention of racism at all. Instead the problem is unfairness, a more generic and softer form of abuse that avoids dealing with the fact that the great majority of White people in Montgomery were racist and capable of being violent and cruel to maintain segregation. Thus we have an adequate picture of neither the courage of Rosa Parks nor the intelligence and resolve of the African American community in the face of racism.

Research into the history of the Montgomery bus boycott, however, reveals some distressing characteristics of this generic story, which misrepresents an organized and carefully planned movement for social change as a spontaneous outburst based upon frustration and anger. The following annotations on "Rosa Was Tired" suggest that we need a new story, one more in line with the truth and directed at showing the organizational intelligence and determination of the African American community in Birmingham, as well as the role of the bus boycott in the larger struggle to desegregate Birmingham and the South.

The Annotated "Rosa Was Tired"

Rosa Parks was a seamstress who was poor. She lived in Montgomery, Alabama, during the 1950s.

Rosa Parks was one of the first women in Montgomery to join the NAACP and was its secretary for years. At the NAACP she worked with E. D. Nixon, vice president of the Brotherhood of Sleeping Car Porters, who was president of the Montgomery NAACP, and learned about union struggles from him. She also worked with the youth division of the NAACP, and she took a youth NAACP group to visit the Freedom Train when it came to Montgomery in 1954. The train, which carried the originals of the U.S. Constitution and the Declaration of Independence, was traveling around the United States promoting the virtues of democracy. Since its visit was a federal project, access to the exhibits could not legally be segregated. Mrs. Parks took advantage of that fact to visit the train. There, Rosa Parks and the members of the youth group mingled freely with European Americans from Montgomery who were also looking at the documents. This overt act of crossing the boundaries of segregation did not endear Rosa Parks to the Montgomery political and social establishment.

Her work as a seamstress in a large department store was secondary to her community work. As she says in an interview in *My Soul Is Rested* by Howard Raines (New York: Bantam, 1978, p. 35), she had "almost a life history of being rebellious against being mistreated because of my color." She was well known to all of the African American leaders in Montgomery for her opposition to segregation, her leadership abilities, and her moral strength. Since 1954 and the Supreme Court's *Brown v. Topeka Board of Education* decision, she had been working on the desegregation of the Montgomery schools. In addition, she was good friends with Clifford and Virginia Durr, European Americans who were well known opponents of segregation. She had also attended an interracial meeting at the Highlander Folk School in Tennessee a few months before the boycott. Highlander was known throughout the South as a radical education center that was overtly planning for the total desegregation of the South, and Rosa Parks was aware of that when she attended the meeting. At that meeting, which dealt with plans for school desegregation in the South, she indicated that she intended to become an active participant in other attempts to break down the barriers of segregation. Finally, Rosa Parks had the active support of her mother and her husband in her civil rights activities. To call Rosa Parks a poor, tired seamstress and not talk about her role as a community leader as well is to turn an organized struggle for freedom into a personal act of frustration. It is a thorough misrepresentation of the Civil Rights movement in Montgomery, Alabama, and an insult to Mrs. Parks as well. Here is a more appropriate way of beginning a children's version of the Montgomery bus boycott:

> It was 1955. Everyone in the African American community in Montgomery, Alabama, knew Rosa Parks. She was a community leader, and people admired her courage. All throughout her life she had opposed prejudice, even if it got her into trouble.

In those days there was still segregation in parts of the United States. That meant that African Americans and European Americans were not allowed to use the same public facilities...

The existence of legalized segregation in the South during the 1950s is integral to the story of the Montgomery bus boycott, yet it is an embarrassment to many school people and difficult to explain to children without accounting for the moral corruption of the majority of the European American community in the South. The sentence I composed is one way of avoiding direct confrontation with the moral issues of segregation. First it says, "In those days there was still segregation" as if segregation were no longer an issue. However, as recently as July 1, 1990, an article by Ron Rapoport of the *Los Angeles Daily News* (reprinted in the Santa Rosa, CA, *Press Democrat*, July 1, 1990) focused on the current segregation of private golf clubs in Birmingham and other parts of the United States. In the article he says:

> It certainly isn't a secret that Shoal Creek Country Club has no black members because, in the words of its founder, Hall Thompson, "that's just not done in Birmingham."
>
> There are lots of places where it's just not done and not just in the South, either. Many of the golf courses that host PGA (Professional Golfers Association) events are restricted and while it may not often become a public issue, that does not mean people are not aware of it.
>
> As for shame, well, that is a commodity that is in short supply as well.
>
> "The country club is our home," Thompson said, "and we pick and choose who we want."

To this day the club still has only one African American member, who has special status as a guest member. Ironically, in 1994 a young African American golfer won a tournament at the club while other African Americans demonstrated outside its gates protesting the club's segregationist policies.

Locating segregation in the past is a way of avoiding dealing with its current manifestations and implying that racism is no longer a major problem in the United States. This is particularly pernicious at a time when overt racism is once again becoming a common phenomenon and when children have to be helped to understand and eliminate it.

Describing integration passively ("there was still segregation" instead of "European Americans segregated facilities so that African Americans couldn't use them") avoids the issue of activist racist activity on the part of some Whites. Since there was legalized segregation in Alabama, and Mrs. Parks was arrested for a violation of the Alabama state law that institutionalized segregation in public facilities, there must have been racists to have passed those laws. Yet they are absent from the narrative, which doesn't talk overtly about racism. The avoidance of direct discussion of what to do about individuals who are racist is all too characteristic of school programs and children's literature.

This avoidance of dealing directly with racism is also evident in the next sentence, which says that "African Americans and European Americans were not allowed to use the same public facilities." It puts African Americans and European Americans on the same footing, as if there were some symmetry and both were punished by the segregation laws. A more appropriate way of describing the situation would be:

> African American people were prevented by law from using the same public facilities as European Americans. In addition, the African American facilities were vastly inferior to the ones made available to European Americans.

Even this rewriting is too generous given the pervasive, brutal, and absolute nature of segregation in the pre-civil rights South. Perhaps the best analogy that could be used here is apartheid, as legalized segregation in the South hardly differed from South Africa's policy of total separation of the races to ensure White dominance.

I've raised the question with a number of educators, both African American and European American, of how to expose children to the reality of segregation and racism. Most of the European American and a few of the African American educators felt that young children do not need to be exposed to the harsh and violent history of segregation in the United States. They worried about the effects such exposure would have on race relations in their classrooms, and especially about provoking rage on the part of African American students. The other educators felt that, given the resurgence of overt racism in the United States these days, allowing rage and anger to come out was the only way African American and European American children could work from the reality of difference and separation toward a common life. They felt that conflict was a positive thing that could be healing when confronted directly, and that avoiding the horrors of racism was just another way of perpetuating them. I agree with this second group and believe that some recasting of the third and fourth sentences of "Rosa Was Tired" is called for:

> In those days Alabama was legally segregated. That means that African American people were prevented by the state law from using the same swimming pools, schools, and other public facilities as European Americans. There also were separate entrances, toilets, and drinking fountains for African Americans and European Americans in places such as bus and train stations. The facilities African Americans were allowed to use were not only separate from the ones European Americans used but were also very inferior. The reason for this was racism, the belief that European Americans were superior to African Americans and that therefore European Americans deserved better facilities.

. . . whenever it was crowded on the city buses African Americans had to give up seats in front to European Americans and move to the back of the bus.

Actually African Americans were never allowed to sit in the front of the bus in the South in those days. The front seats were *reserved* for European Americans. Between five and ten rows back the "Colored" section began. When the front of the bus filled up, African Americans seated in the "Colored" section had to give up their seats and move toward the back of the bus. Thus, for example, an elderly African American woman would have to give up her seat to a European American teenage male at the peril of being arrested. Consistent with the comments I've been making so far, and with the truth of the experience of segregation, this sentence should be expanded as follows:

> In those days public buses were divided into two sections, one at the front for European Americans, which was supposed to be "for Whites only." From five to ten rows back the section for African Americans began. That part of the bus was called the "Colored" section.
>
> Whenever it was crowded on the city buses African American people were forced to give up seats in the "Colored" section to European Americans and move to the back of the bus. For example, an elderly African American woman would have to give up her seat to a European American teenage male. If she refused she could be arrested for breaking the segregation laws.

One day on her way home from work Rosa was tired and sat down in the front of the bus.

Rosa Parks did not sit in the front of the bus. She sat in the front row of the "Colored" section. When the bus got crowded she refused to give up her seat in the "Colored" section to a European American. It is important to point this out, as it indicates quite clearly that it was not her intent, on that day, to break the segregation laws.

At this point the story lapses into the familiar and refers to Rosa Parks as "Rosa." The question of whether to use the first name for historical characters in a factual story is complicated. One argument in favor of doing so is that young children will more readily identify with characters who are presented in a personalized and familiar way. However, given that it was a sanctioned social practice in the South during the time of the story for European Americans to call African American adults by their first names as a way of reinforcing the African Americans' inferior status (African Americans could never call European Americans by their first names without breaking the social code of segregation), it seems unwise to use that practice in the story.

In addition, it's reasonable to assume that Rosa Parks was not any more tired on that one day than on other days. She worked at an exhausting full-time job and was also active full-time in the community. To emphasize her being tired is another way of saying that her defiance of segregation was an accidental result of her fatigue and consequent short temper on that particular day. However, rage is not a one-day thing, and Rosa Parks acted with full knowledge of what she was doing.

It is more respectful and historically accurate to make these changes:

> December 1, 1955, on her way home from work, Rosa Parks took the bus as usual. She sat down in the front row of the "Colored" section.

As the bus got crowded she was asked to give up her seat to a European American man, and she refused. The bus driver told her she had to go to the back of the bus, and she still refused to move. It was a hot day, and she was tired and angry, and became very stubborn.

The driver called a policeman, who arrested Rosa.

Rosa Parks described her experiences with buses in her own words (*My Soul Is Rested*):

> I had problems with bus drivers over the years because I didn't see fit to pay my money into the front and then go around to the back. Sometimes bus drivers wouldn't permit me to get on the bus, and I had been evicted from the bus. But, as I say, there had been incidents over the years. One of the things that made this . . . (incident) . . . get so much publicity was the fact that the police were called in and I was placed under arrest. See, if I had just been evicted from the bus and he hadn't placed me under arrest or had any charges brought against me, it probably could have been just another incident. (p. 31)

More recently, in *Voices of Freedom* by Henry Hampton and Steve Fayer (New York: Bantam, 1990), she described her thoughts that day in the following way:

Having to take a certain section [on a bus] because of your race was humiliating, but having to stand up because a particular driver wanted to keep a white person from having to stand was, to my mind, most inhumane.

More than seventy-five, between eighty-five and I think ninety, percent of the patronage of the buses were black people, because more white people could own and drive their own cars than blacks. I happened to be the secretary of the Montgomery branch of the NAACP as well as the NAACP Youth Council adviser. Many cases did come to my attention that nothing came out of because the person that was abused would be too intimidated to sign an affidavit, or to make a statement. Over the years, I had had my own problems with the bus drivers. In fact, some did tell me not to ride their buses if I felt that I was too important to go to the back door to get on. One had evicted me from the bus in 1943, which did not cause anything more than just a passing glance.

On December 1, 1955, I had finished my day's work as a tailor's assistant in the Montgomery Fair department store and I was on my way home. There was one vacant seat on the Cleveland Avenue bus, which I took, alongside a man and two women across the aisle. There were still a few vacant seats in the white section in the front, of course. We went to the next stop without being disturbed. On the third, the front seats were occupied and this one man, a white man, was standing. The driver asked us to stand up and let him have those seats, and when none of us moved at his first words, he said, "You all make it light on yourselves and let me have those seats." And the man who was sitting next to the window stood up, and I made room for him to pass by me. The two women across the aisle stood up and moved out. When the driver saw me still sitting, he asked if I was going to stand up and I said, "No, I'm not."

And he said, "Well, if you don't stand up, I'm going to call the police and have you arrested."

I said, "You may do that."

He did get off the bus, and I still stayed where I was. Two policemen came on the bus. One of the policemen asked me if the bus driver had asked me to stand and I said yes.

He said, "Why don't you stand up?"

And I asked him, "Why do you push us around?"

He said, "I do not know, but the law is the law and you're under arrest." (pp. 19, 20)

Mere anger and stubbornness could not account for the clear resolve with which Rosa Parks acted. Nor was she, as Robert Fulghum says in the selection from his book quoted at the beginning of this issue, "Not an activist or a radical. Just a quiet, conservative, churchgoing woman with a nice family and a decent job as a seamstress." She knew what she was doing, understood the consequences, and was prepared to confront segregation head on at whatever sacrifice she had to make. A more accurate account of the event, taking into consideration Rosa Parks's past history, might be:

> As the bus got crowded the driver demanded that she give up her seat to a European American man, and move to the back of the bus. This was not the first time that this had happened to Rosa Parks. In the past she had refused to move, and the driver had simply put her off the bus. Mrs. Parks hated segregation, and along with many other African American people, refused to obey many of its unfair rules. On this day she refused to do what the bus driver demanded.
>
> The bus driver commanded her once more to go to the back of the bus and she stayed in her seat, looking straight ahead and not moving an inch. He got angry at her and became very stubborn. He called a policeman, who arrested Mrs. Parks.

When other African Americans in Montgomery heard this they became angry too, so they decided to refuse to ride the buses until everyone was allowed to ride together. They boycotted the buses.

The connection between Rosa Parks's arrest and the boycott is a mystery in most accounts of what happened in Montgomery. Community support for the boycott is portrayed as being instantaneous and miraculously effective the very day after Mrs. Parks was arrested. Things don't happen that way, and it is an insult to the intelligence and courage of the African American community in Montgomery to turn their planned resistance to segregation into a spontaneous emotional response. The actual situation was more interesting and complex. Not only Rosa Parks had defied the bus segregation laws in the past: According to E. D. Nixon, in the three months preceding Mrs. Parks's arrest at least three other African American people had been arrested in Montgomery for refusing to give up their bus seats to European American people. In each case, Nixon and other people in leadership positions in the African

American community in Montgomery investigated the background of the person arrested. They were looking for someone who had the respect of the community and the strength to deal with the racist police force as well as all the publicity that would result from being at the center of a bus boycott. This leads to the most important point left out in popularized accounts of the Montgomery bus boycott: the boycott had been planned and organized before Rosa Parks was arrested. It was an event waiting to take place, and that is why it could be mobilized so quickly. Rosa Parks's arrest brought it about because she was part of the African American leadership in Montgomery and was trusted not to cave in under the pressure everyone knew she would be exposed to, including threats to her life.

But the story goes back even farther than that. There was an African American women's organization in Montgomery called the Women's Political Council (WPC). It was headed those days by Jo Ann Gibson Robinson, who was a professor of English at Alabama State University in Montgomery, an all-African American university. In 1949 Ms. Gibson was put off a bus in Montgomery for refusing to move from her seat in the fifth row of an almost empty bus to the back of the bus. She and other women in Montgomery resolved to do something about bus segregation. As she says in her book *The Montgomery Bus Boycott and the Women Who Started It: The Memoir of Jo Ann Gibson Robinson* (Knoxville: University of Tennessee Press, 1987), "It was during the period of 1949–1955 that the Women's Political Council of Montgomery—founded in 1946 with Dr. Mary Burks as president and headed from 1950 on by me—prepared to stage a bus boycott when the time was ripe and the people were ready. The right time came in 1955." (p. 17)

This story of collective decision making, willed risk, and coordinated action is more dramatic than the story of an angry individual who sparked a demonstration; it has more to teach children who themselves may have to organize and act collectively against oppressive forces in the future. Here's one way to tell this complex story to young children:

> Mrs. Parks was not the first African American person to be arrested in Montgomery for refusing to move to the back of the bus. In the months before her refusal, at least three other people were arrested for the same reason. In fact, African American leaders in Montgomery were planning to overcome segregation. One way they wanted to do this was to have every African American person boy-

cott the buses. Since most of the bus riders in the city were African American, the buses would go broke if they refused to let African Americans and European Americans ride the buses as equals.

From 1949 right up to the day Mrs. Parks refused to move, the Women's Political Council of Montgomery prepared to stage a bus boycott because of how African Americans were treated on the bus. African American people in Montgomery were ready to support the boycott. They were just waiting for the time to be ripe. Nineteen fifty-five was the time.

However, none of the people who were arrested before Mrs. Parks was were leaders. She was a leader, and the day she was arrested the leadership called a meeting at the Dexter Avenue Baptist Church. They decided to begin their refusal to ride the buses the next morning. They knew Mrs. Parks had the courage to deal with the pressure of defying segregation and would not yield even if her life was threatened.

The next day the Montgomery bus boycott began.

The boycott, which was led by Martin Luther King Jr., succeeded. Now African Americans and European Americans can ride the buses together in Montgomery. Rosa Parks was a very brave person.

The boycott was planned by the WPC, E. D. Nixon, and others in Montgomery. Martin Luther King Jr. was a new member of the community. He had just taken over the Dexter Avenue Baptist Church, and when Nixon told him that Rosa Parks's arrest was just what everybody was waiting for to kick off a bus boycott and assault the institution of segregation, King was at first reluctant. However, the community people chose him to lead, and he accepted their call. The boycott lasted 381 inconvenient days, something not usually mentioned in children's books. It did succeed and was one of the events that sparked the entire Civil Rights movement. People who had been planning an overt attack on segregation for years took that victory as a sign that the time was ripe, even though the people involved in the Montgomery boycott did not themselves anticipate such results. Here's one possible way to convey this to children:

> There was a young new minister in Montgomery those days. His name was Martin Luther King Jr. People in the community felt that he was a special person and asked him to lead the boycott. At first he wasn't sure. He worried about the violence that might result from the boycott. However, he quickly made up his mind that it was time

to destroy segregation and accepted the people's call for him to be their leader.

The Montgomery bus boycott lasted 381 days. For over a year the African American people of Montgomery, Alabama, stayed off the buses. Some walked to work, others rode bicycles or shared car rides. It was very hard for them, but they knew that what they were doing was very important for all African American people in the South.

The boycott succeeded, and by the end of 1956 African Americans and European Americans could ride the buses in Montgomery as equals. However, the struggle for the complete elimination of segregation had just begun.

We all owe a great deal to the courage and intelligence of Rosa Parks and the entire African American community of Montgomery, Alabama. They took risks to make democracy work for all of us.

CONCLUDING THOUGHTS

What remains, then, is to retitle the story. The revised version is still about Rosa Parks, but it is also about the African American people of Montgomery, Alabama. It takes the usual, individualized version of the Rosa Parks tale and puts it in the context of a coherent, community-based social struggle. This does not diminish Rosa Parks in any way. It places her, however, in the midst of a consciously planned movement for social change, and reminds me of the freedom song "We shall not be moved," for it was precisely Rosa Parks's and the community's refusal to be moved that made the boycott possible. For that reason the new title, "She Would Not Be Moved: The Story of Rosa Parks and the Montgomery Bus Boycott" makes sense.

As it turns out, my retelling of the story of Rosa Parks and the Montgomery bus boycott is not the only recent one. In 1990, thirty-five years after the event, we finally have a full, moving, and historically accurate 124-page retelling of the story written for young people. The book, *Rosa Parks: The Movement Organizes* by Kai Friese (Englewood Cliffs, NJ: Silver Burdett, 1990), is one of nine volumes in a series edited by the scholar Eldon Morris entitled *The History of the Civil Rights Movement*. Other volumes in the series, such as those about Ella Baker and Fannie Lou Hamer, also provide a fuller, more accurate look at people's struggles during the Civil Rights movement of the 1960s than has been available to young people until now. These volumes are gifts to all of us from a number of African American scholars who have reclaimed history from the distortions and omissions of years of irresponsible writing for children about the Civil Rights movement. They are models of how history and biography can directly confront racial conflict and illuminate social struggle. This is particularly true of the Rosa Parks volume, which takes us up to date in Mrs. Parks's life and informs us that she remained active over the years, working for social and economic justice in Congressman John Conyer's office in Detroit.

The book, which credits all the people involved in making the Montgomery boycott possible, provides a portrait of a community mobilized for justice. It also leaves us with a sense of the struggle that still needs to be waged to eliminate racism in the United States.

Rosa Parks has also written an autobiography (with Jim Haskins), which presents a more personal version of the story given here.

When the story of the Montgomery bus boycott is told merely as a tale of a single heroic person, it leaves children hanging. Not everyone is a hero or heroine. Of course, the idea that only special people can create change is useful if you want to prevent mass movements and keep change from happening. Not every child can be a Rosa Parks, but everyone can imagine her- or himself as a participant in the boycott. As a tale of a social movement and a community effort to overthrow injustice, the Rosa Parks story as I've tried to rewrite it and as Kai Friese has told it opens the possibility of every child identifying her- or himself as an activist, as someone who can help make justice happen. And it is that kind of empowerment that people in the United States desperately need.

Appendix I

The following quotes are taken from recent children's books and school textbooks. The publication date of the earliest of them is 1976; the rest were published in their current form in the 1980s. However, two of the children's books were copyrighted in 1969 and reissued in the 1980s with new illustrations. No attempt was made in these two cases to update the material in the books.

The sample of quotes included is representative of dozens I've read, and cumulatively represents all the different aspects of the Rosa Parks myth I portrayed in "Rosa Was Tired." Some of the other texts and the specific lines that relate to my text are listed at the end of this appendix. The passages quoted more fully here are from the most progressive texts and trade books I've found. I have avoided citing texts no longer in print.

1. From Valerie Schloredt, *Martin Luther King Jr: America's Great Nonviolent Leader in the Struggle for Human Rights* (Harrisburg, PA: Morehouse Publishing, 1990).

> On the evening of Dec. 1, 1955, a black lady named Rosa Parks left the downtown department store where she worked as a seamstress and walked to the bus stop to catch the bus that would take her home.

The book goes on to describe what happened when Mrs. Parks refused to move to the back of the bus:

> Mrs. Parks was tired. She had a long, hard day. . . . Something snapped in Mrs. Parks at that moment. Perhaps the patience with which she had endured years of subservience and insult. . . . Mrs. Parks didn't look like a person to challenge the law of Montgomery. She was a quiet looking lady, wearing small steel rimmed spectacles; but like thousands of other black people who rode the buses day after day, she was weary of being treated with such contempt.
>
> Much later she was asked if she had planned her protest. "No," she answered. "I was just plain tired, and my feet hurt."
>
> Mrs. Parks' patience had given way, had she but known it, at the best possible moment. (pp. 19, 20)

2. Here is the Random House version for first- to third-graders from James T. Kay, *Meet Martin Luther King Jr.* (New York: Random House, Step-up Books, 1969), reprinted with new cover in 1989.

> On Dec. 1, 1955, a woman named Rosa Parks did something about the Jim Crow buses.
>
> Mrs. Parks was black. She worked in a department store. That evening she climbed the bus and sat down.
>
> Each time the bus stopped, more people got on. Soon no seats were left in the white part of the bus.
>
> At the next stop some white people got on. The driver got up and walked over to Mrs. Parks. He told her to give her seat to a white woman.

But Rosa Parks was tired. She did something she had never done before. She just stayed in her seat. . . .

Black people all over the city heard about Rosa Parks. They were very angry. They were mad at the Jim Crow laws. They were mad at the police. They were mad at the bus company. But what could they do?

Then one man said, "Why don't we boycott the buses?" This meant that all the black people would stop riding the buses. Soon the bus company would lose money. Maybe then the owners would be fair to blacks. (not paged)

3. This selection is from Dharathula H. Millender's *Martin Luther King, Jr.: Young Man with a Dream* (New York: Bobbs-Merrill, 1969; Macmillan, Alladin Books, 1986). It is one of the finest of the older children's books about the Civil Rights movment.

Things came to a head over bus segregation on December 1, 1955. Mrs. Rosa Parks, an attractive negro seamstress, boarded a bus in downtown Montgomery. This was the same bus she had boarded many times after a hard day's work. Today she was tired and eager to get off her aching feet. Accordingly she sat down in the first seat in the Negro section behind the section reserved for white passengers. . . .

At first the driver was surprised (when she refused to move) wondering whether he had heard correctly. When Mrs. Parks clung to her seat, however, and held her head proudly in the air, he realized that he was facing trouble. Accordingly, he stopped his bus, called the police and had her arrested. Her arrest attracted wide attention because she was one of the most respected people in the Negro community. It helped to start a Negro revolt not only in Montgomery but all across the nation. (pp. 148–9)

4. This is from the upper elementary grades social studies textbook *The United States and the Other Americas* by Allan King, Ida Dennis, and Florence Potter, in the Macmillan Social Studies Series (New York: Macmillan, 1982).

In 1955 Rosa Parks, a black, refused to give up her bus seat to a white in Montgomery, Alabama. She was arrested because of this. Other blacks, led by Dr. Martin Luther King Jr., of Atlanta, Georgia, refused to ride the city buses. The following year a federal court ruled that segregated buses were no longer allowed. (p. 141)

In the teachers' edition the following instructions are given to teachers:

> Have the pupils read the rest of page 413. Draw their attention to the photograph of Rosa Parks. Explain that on December 1, 1955, Rosa Parks boarded a bus in Montgomery, Alabama. Her arms were full of groceries, so she sat in the front row of the section of the bus in which blacks were permitted to sit. As the bus filled up, more white people got on, and the bus driver told Rosa to give up her seat to a white person. Rosa looked out the window and pretended not to hear him. She refused to give up her seat, and because of this she was arrested. In protest against her arrest, the black people of Montgomery refused to ride the bus. They formed car pools, walked, rode mules and horses and buggies. On April 23, 1956, the Supreme Court declared that state and local laws that required segregation of buses were unconstitutional. (p. 413)

5. This is taken from Allan O. Kownslar and William R. Fielder's *Inquiring About American History* (New York: Holt, Rinehart and Winston, 1976), in the Holt Databank System. This is a "modern" series based on inquiry and is considered too liberal for many school districts. It is for upper elementary and junior high students.

> For the black citizens of Montgomery, Alabama, some of the "separate but equal" laws had been changed by 1955. . . . But, in spite of these changes, many people still refused to treat blacks and whites equally. Rosa Parks, a black woman who lived in Montgomery in 1955, had to deal with this problem.
>
> One evening, Rosa Parks was coming home from work on a Montgomery city bus. She had been working hard all day at her job in a downtown department store. Rosa was quite tired. She took a seat toward the back of the bus, where black passengers normally sat. The bus began to fill quickly. As whites got on, they took what seats there were, and soon the bus was full.
>
> Rosa realized that some of the blacks would be asked to give up their seats and move to the back of the bus. They would be asked to stand so that white passengers could sit. She felt that this was unfair. Why should she have to move?
>
> Suddenly the driver turned and asked her, and some other blacks, to move to the rear of the bus. Rosa argued with the driver, but he still insisted that she leave her seat and stand in the back. Rosa paused. She had to make a decision quickly. Should she give up her seat or remain seated?

What would you have done if you had been Rosa Parks? What do you think she did?

Rosa Parks made her choice. She decided to remain seated on the bus. Her action led to the Montgomery Bus Boycott—and eventually, to a Supreme Court ruling against the separation of blacks and whites on all buses. (p. 301)

6. This selection is from another upper elementary text, *The United States and Its Neighbors* by Timothy Helmus, Val Arnsdorf, Edgar Toppin, and Norman Pounds (Morristown, NJ: Silver Burdett, 1984), in the series *The World and Its People.*

> Dr. King gained nationwide fame in Montgomery, Alabama, in 1955. At that time blacks had to sit in the back of public buses. But one day a quiet woman named Rosa Parks decided to sit in the "whites only" part of the bus. She was arrested. Dr. King led a boycott of Montgomery buses to protest her arrest. People who supported Dr. King would not use the buses until anyone could sit wherever she or he pleased. The boycott worked. (p. 248)

Finally, here is a list of quotes from a sampling of texts for all grade levels dealing with Rosa Parks and the Montgomery bus boycott. I've only quoted eighteen of the dozens of books consulted, though I think the unity of their tale comes across quite clearly. The word *racism* was not used in any of them.

1. Karen McAuley et al., *The United States Past to Present,* Teacher's Ed. (Lexington, MA: D. C. Heath, 1987), p. 405. Grade 5.
"It had been a long, hard day and she was tired."

2. Susan Williams McKay, *The World of Mankind* (Chicago: Follet Publishing, 1973), p. 221. Grade 3.
"Mrs. Parks sat alone. She was tired. She decided not to move."

3. *The United States: Its History and Neighbors,* Teacher's Ed. (Orlando, FL: Harcourt Brace Jovanovich, 1988), p. 507. Grade 5.
"On Dec. 1, 1955, Rosa Parks sank wearily to her seat on the bus in Montgomery, Alabama. . . .

"As the bus filled up, Rosa Parks was asked to give up her seat. She refused. The bus driver called the police, and she was taken to jail."

4. Leonard C. Wood et al., *America: Its People and Values*, Teacher's Ed. 1985, p. 721. Junior High.
"On that day a black seamstress named Rosa Parks refused to give up her seat in the white section of the bus. . . .

"There as in many other parts of the south, local laws kept public places strictly segregated. Restaurants, businesses, and all forms of public transportation had separate sections for blacks and whites."

5. Allan O. Kownslar et al., *Inquiring About American History* (New York: Holt, Rinehart and Winston, 1976) p. 301. Grade 5.
"One evening, Rosa Parks was coming home from work on a Montgomery city bus. She had been working hard all day at her job . . . Rosa was quite tired . . . ."

"Suddenly, the driver turned and asked her, and some other blacks, to move to the rear of the bus. Rosa argued with the driver . . ."

6. JoAnn Cangemi, *Our History*, 1983, pp. 388–89. Grade 5.
"In 1955, a black woman named Rosa Parks sat down in the front of the bus in Montgomery, Alabama. Parks refused to get up from the seat so that a white person could sit down and she was arrested."

"Angry about the arrest, Montgomery blacks refused to ride city buses."
"The bus boycott was led by Dr. Martin Luther King, Jr."

7. Beverly J. Armento et al., *This Is My Country* (Boston: Houghton Mifflin, 1991) p. 98. Grade 4.
"She was tired and her feet hurt"

"At that time, black and white people had to sit in separate sections on the bus. Other places were divided too, such as restrooms, waiting rooms, movie theatres and restaurants."

8. Henry F. Graff, *America: The Glorious Republic*, vol. 1, 1985, pp. 717–18. Jr./Sr. High.
"The next day the 50,000 black citizens of Montgomery began a bus boy-

cott of the city's buses: choosing to walk rather than ride under humiliating conditions."

9. Henry F. Graff, *America: The Glorious Republic*, vol. 2, 1986, pp. 349–50. Jr./Sr. High.
". . . a seamstress named Rosa Parks took a courageous and fateful step."
"The next day the 50,000 black citizens of Montgomery began a boycott of city buses."

10. John Edward Wiltz, *The Search for Identity: Modern American History* (Philadelphia: J. B. Lippincott, 1973), p. 684. Jr. High.
"When Mrs. Parks, a small, soft-spoken woman boarded the Cleveland Avenue bus she was tired and her feet hurt."

11. Beverly Jeanne Armento et al., *Living in Our Country* (River Forest, IL: Laidlaw Brothers, 1988) pp. 417–18. Grade 5.
"In Montgomery, Alabama, a black woman was arrested for using a seat in the front of a bus."
"For this reason many black people refused to ride the buses in Montgomery."

12. Glen M. Linden et al., *Legacy of Freedom: A History of the United States*, 1986, p. 670. Jr./Sr. High.
"Tired after a long day's work, Mrs. Parks boarded a bus for home and refused to give up her seat to a white passenger when asked to do so by the bus driver."
"The leaders of Montgomery's black community were outraged. Almost at once, they organized a boycott of the Mongomery transit system."

13. Ernest R. May, *A Proud Nation*, Teacher's Ed. (Evanston, IL: McDougal, Littell, 1983), p. 691. Jr. High.
"On Dec. 1, Rosa Parks, a black woman, refused to give up her seat in the front of a bus to a white person. She had simply worked hard all day, Parks said, and her feet hurt."

14. Alma Graham et al., *United States: Our Nation and Neighbors* (New

York: McGraw-Hill, 1980, p. 340. Grade 5.
"The bus boycott was led by Dr. Martin Luther King Jr."

15. George Vuicich et al., *United States*, 1983, p. 322. Grade 5.
"In 1955, a black woman, Rosa Parks, refused to give up her seat on a bus in Montgomery, Alabama. She was arrested. Some people became determined to do something. Blacks in Montgomery began a boycott of the city's buses."
    "The bus boycott was led by Dr. Martin Luther King, Jr., . . ."

16. Henry F. Graff et al., *The Promise of Democracy: The Grand Experiment* (Chicago: Rand McNally, 1978), pp. 365–66. Jr./Sr. High.
" . . . in many southern communities, black people had to sit at the back of the city buses."
    " . . . and she was tired."

17. Roger M. Berg, *Social Studies* (Glenview, IL: Scott, Foresman, 1979), p. 335. Grade 5.
"In some cities, blacks were forced to ride in separate parts of buses. In 1955, in Montgomery, Alabama, Rosa Parks wanted to sit in a part of a public bus set aside for whites. She was arrested. The black people of Montgomery refused to ride the city buses until they could sit where they wanted."

18. Richard H. Loftin et al., *Our Country's Communities* (Morristown, NJ: Silver Burdett and Ginn), 1988, p. 246, Grade 3.
"One day a black woman named Rosa Parks got on a bus and found the back seats filled. She had been working all day and was tired. She sat down in another seat and was arrested."
    "With Dr. King as their leader, the black people of Montgomery refused to ride on the bus until they had the same rights as the other riders."
    "They did as he (King) said and finally won out."

Appendix II

Here is the complete text of "She Would Not Be Moved: The Story of Rosa Parks and the Montgomery Bus Boycott."

It was 1955. Everyone in the African American community in Montgomery, Alabama, knew Rosa Parks. She was a community leader, and people admired her courage. All throughout her life she had opposed prejudice, even if it got her into trouble with European American people.

In those days Alabama was legally segregated. That means that African American people were prevented by the state law from using the same swimming pools, schools, and other public facilities as European Americans. There also were separate entrances, toilets, and drinking fountains for African Americans and European Americans in places such as bus and train stations.

The facilities African Americans were allowed to use were not only separate from the ones European Americans used but were also very inferior. The reason for this was racism, the belief that European Americans were superior to African Americans and that therefore European Americans deserved better facilities.

In those days public buses were divided into two sections, one at the front for European Americans, which was supposed to be "for Whites only." From five to ten rows back the section for African Americans began. That part of the bus was called the "Colored" section.

Whenever it was crowded on the city buses African American people were forced to give up seats in the "Colored" section to European Americans and move to the back of the bus. For example, an elderly African American woman would have to give up her seat to a European American teenage male. If she refused she could be arrested for breaking the segregation laws.

December 1, 1955 on her way home from work, Rosa Parks took the bus as usual. She sat down in the front row of the "Colored" section. As the bus got crowded the driver demanded that she give up her seat to a European American man, and move to the back of the bus. This was not the first time that this had happened to Rosa Parks. In the past she had refused to move, and the driver had simply put her off the bus. Mrs. Parks hated segregation, and along with many other African American people, refused to obey many of its unfair rules. On this day, she refused to do what the bus driver demanded.

The bus driver commanded her once more to go to the back of the bus and she stayed in her seat, looking straight ahead and not moving an inch. It was a hot day and the driver was angry and became very stubborn. He called a policeman, who arrested Mrs. Parks.

Mrs. Parks was not the first African American person to be arrested in Montgomery for refusing to move to the back of the bus. In the months before her refusal, at least three other people were arrested for the same reason. In fact, African American leaders in Montgomery were planning to overcome segregation. One way they wanted to do this was to have every African American person boycott the buses. Since most of the bus riders in the city were African American, the buses would go broke if they refused to let African Americans and European Americans ride the buses as equals.

From 1949 right up to the day Mrs. Parks refused to move, the Women's Political Council of Montgomery prepared to stage a bus boycott because of how African Americans were treated on the bus. They were just waiting for the time to be ripe. Nineteen fifty-five was the time.

However, none of the people who were arrested before Mrs. Parks was were leaders. She was a leader, and the day she was arrested the leadership called a meeting at the Dexter Avenue Baptist Church. They decided to begin their refusal to ride the buses the next morning. They knew Mrs. Parks had the courage to deal with the pressure of defying segregation and would not yield even if her life was threatened.

The next day the Montgomery bus boycott began.

There was a young new minister in Montgomery those days. His name was Martin Luther King, Jr. People in the community felt that he was a special person and asked him to lead the boycott. At first he wasn't sure. He worried about the violence that might result from the boycott. However, he quickly made up his mind that it was time to destroy segregation and accepted the people's call for him to be their leader.

The Montgomery bus boycott lasted 381 days. For over a year the African American people of Montgomery, Alabama, stayed off the buses. Some walked to work, others rode bicycles or shared car rides. It was very inconvenient for them, but they knew that what they were doing was very important for all African American people in the South.

The boycott succeeded, and by the end of 1956 African Americans and European Americans could ride the buses in Montgomery as equals. However, the struggle for the complete elimination of segregation had just begun.

We all owe a great deal to the courage and intelligence of Rosa Parks and the entire African American community of Montgomery, Alabama. They took risks to make democracy work for all of us.

A Plea for Radical
Children's Literature

A grave I accidentally discovered in Boston several years ago tempted me to write a novel for young people. The graveyard contains the remains of great names in our history such as Crispus Attucks and Samuel Adams, yet it was the small plot that contains the remains of Christopher Snider that set me to fantasize a life and think of writing a story about it. According to a plaque at his graveside, Snider was killed on February 22, 1770, at the age of twelve "the innocent first victim in the struggle between the colonists and the crown which resulted in Independence." Was Christopher just caught in a skirmish, and was he really the first victim? Was he a young revolutionary? Did he hear shots and feel a need to get involved in the action, or was he on his way home or to work? What did he look like? Who were his parents? Were they rich or poor? Colonists or Loyalists? Was there an available history of the Snider family in Boston during the 1770s? The name sounded German. Why were they in Boston? And what happened in Boston on February 22, 1770? How did Christopher die? Was he shot, and if so was it intentional? I noticed that Christopher was killed on George Washington's birthday, his thirty-eighth, it turns out. What was Washington doing that day? Was there any way to tie these together?

Story possibilities ran through my mind, and upon arriving home I began to do some research. According to *The Growth of the American Republic* by Morrison and Commanger, vol. 1, Fifth Ed. (Oxford University Press, 1962, pp. 168–70), in January 1770, New York City "was the scene of a serious riot—British troops cut down a liberty pole erected by the radicals and piled the pieces in front of the Sons of Liberty headquarters. A fight followed on Gordon Hill, the mob using clubs and staves against the soldiers' cutlasses and bayonets, and one citizen was killed. This affair is New York's claim for having been the scene of the 'first bloodshed' of the Revolution." The Boston Massacre took place on March 5,

1770. Morrison and Commager say, "The presence of British red-coats in Boston was a standing invitation to disorder. Antagonism between citizens and soldiery flared up in the so-called 'Boston Massacre' of 5 March 1770. A snowballing of the red-coats Bostonians degenerated into a mob attack, someone gave the order to fire, and four lay dead in the snow."

Further research revealed that snowballing was not simply innocent harassment of the British troops. The snowballs were made by packing snow around stones, and they were lethal. So, could Christopher have thrown a loaded snowball and gotten shot? Or been mistaken for someone doing it? Was he an innocent victim, or was he involved in a community-wide intimidation of the troops?

Snowballing was not foreign to me. When I was Christopher's age I was involved in battles between Irish and Jewish kids in the Bronx. Our main weapon was a snowball made by packing snow around conkers, burnt coal ash we picked out of the garbage cans. I remember broken noses and bloody heads.

Visions of snowballing in Boston reminded me further of pictures of Palestinian children stoning Israeli troops. Was there something similar in the violent political activities of young people during the American Revolution and the Intifada?

Over the years of my involvement in social struggle, from the resistance to HUAC and the McCarthy committee through the Civil Rights and anti-war movements to current struggles over racism and the environment, I have been struck by the active role young people have played and by the lack of credit they have received for their actions. In high school I was involved with student groups that defended our teachers when they were called before the McCarthy committee, their peers having abandoned them. During the Civil Rights movement, young people often led the way. Think, for example, of the youngsters who integrated the schools in the South, of the sit-ins, of SNCC, and, most dramatically, of the demonstrations initiated by African American children as young as eight and nine in Montgomery, Alabama. Many historical accounts attribute these last acts to the leadership of Martin Luther King Jr., but in fact, he supported the children's demonstrations only after the children had already been out on the street.

Christopher Snider got me thinking about young activists and their stories, and I began to read books for young adults that dealt with social issues and young activists, or at least young people who were involved in social struggle. I quickly found out that in young adult literature, problem books are in. There are adolescent novels about incest, confronting racism, domestic violence, divorce, and AIDS. I read one about the cruelty of sending grandparents to old folks homes and another about death from cancer. There are books on gang life, prison, teenage parenthood, homelessness, and the experiences of young people during the Civil Rights movement of the 1960s. As a whole these books give the impression of young adults as an embattled class, facing the problems of a society under stress. Still, the books project hope or success—hope in the shape of better things to come for the heroine or hero in the future, and success in that one or more of the main figures finds a way to make it to wealth or power.

The range and variety of these books are quite different from what was available to me as a child in the late 1940s and as a beginning teacher in the 1960s. Yet despite all the personal and social sensitivity represented in young adult literature today, there is still an almost total absence of books, fiction or nonfiction, that question the economic and social structure of our society and the values of capitalism.

Books that deal with poor people concern the efforts of individual youngsters or families to escape poverty, but they never depict collective struggles to overcome poverty. Books on social movements center on leaders and on participants who have performed individually heroic actions, not on the building of movements and the power of people united in struggle. Books on old age focus on the need for families to take care of the old even at high economic and personal cost, but never on the effort to make access to health care a right. Gang books talk about truces and individuals getting out of the gangs to pursue more meaningful activities, but not about the rage of gang members and struggles to remake communities so that gangs do not become an attractive way of life. And the few books that deal with problems in the corporate world deal with corrupt or troubled individuals and not with the system of profit and competition that breeds corruption and creates angst. Though there is a great deal of compassionate, liberal literature for young adults on sensitive issues, it is hard to find any radical literature on the same topics.

This is not a new concern. In 1939 George Orwell published the essay "Boys' Weeklies," in which he asked: "Why is there no such thing as a left-wing boys paper?" (*Collected Essays,* p. 115). Orwell's question, which seems dated now, was much larger than that specific reference to weekly magazines (the equivalent of comic books). Orwell wondered why the most effective writing for young people was infused with the mythology of elitism, individualism, and capitalism. Why, he asked, are there so many exciting and well-written books that extol fame and fortune, and define success as defending capitalism, affirming individualism, or conquering the enemies of the status quo, and so few that portray working-class struggles, or the struggles of other groups of people for equity and justice?

Orwell's question and my current reading set me on a quest. Are there any good books for young people that are not written from the perspective of the virtues of individualism, competition, and capitalism? Are there any about social, economic, and racial struggles that do not end up, even in triumph, having the heroines and heroes conform to the norms of our economic system? Are there any good tales about young people involved in collective struggles for social and economic justice? Stories that do not celebrate wealth? In other words, are there any books written for young people that question the economic and social basis of our society?

In his essay, Orwell imagines what a left-wing boys' weekly, and, by extension, radical fiction for young people, might be like, and speculates on why it would be dogmatic and uninteresting literature:

> It is so horribly easy to imagine what a left-wing boys' paper would be like, if it existed. I remember in 1920 or 1921 some optimistic person handing round Communist tracts among a crowd of public-school boys. The tract I received was of the question-and-answer kind:
> Q. "Can a Boy Communist be a Boy Scout, Comrade?"
> A. "No, Comrade."
> Q. "Why, Comrade?"
> A. "Because, Comrade, a Boy Scout must salute the Union Jack, which is the symbol of tyranny and oppression." Etc. etc.
>
> Now, suppose that at this moment somebody started a left-wing paper deliberately aimed at boys of twelve or fourteen. I do not suggest that the whole of its contents would be exactly like the tract I have quoted above, but does anyone doubt that they would be something like it? Inevitably such a paper would either consist of dreary uplift or it would be under Communist influence . . . in either case no normal boy would ever look at it.

But it does not follow that it is impossible. There is no clear reason why every adventure story should necessarily be mixed up with snobbishness and gutter patriotism. For, after all, the stories in the Hotspur and the Modern Boy are not Conservative tracts; they are merely adventure stories with a Conservative bias. It is fairly easy to imagine the process being reversed. It is possible, for instance, to imagine a paper as thrilling and lively as the Hotspur, but with subject-matter and "ideology" a little more up to date. It is even possible (though this raises other difficulties) to imagine a women's paper at the same literary level as the Oracle, dealing in approximately the same kind of story, but taking rather more account of the realities of working class life.

Orwell did have some examples in mind:

In the last years of the Spanish monarchy there was a large output in Spain of left-wing novelettes, some of them evidently of anarchist origin. Unfortunately at the time when they were appearing I did not see their social significance, and I lost the collection of them that I had, but no doubt copies would still be procurable. In get-up and style of story they were very similar to the English four penny novelette, except that their inspiration was "left." If, for instance, a story described police pursuing anarchists through the mountains, it would be from the point of view of the anarchist and not of the police. . . . All the usual paraphernalia is there—heroic fight against odds, escape at the last moment, shots of galloping horses, love interest, comic relief.

For the past ten years I have searched for these anarchist books and have not been able to find any of them. There is a vast, almost empty field when it comes to progressive fiction for young people. Orwell describes some of the problems himself:

Here several difficult problems present themselves. . . . In England, popular imaginative literature is a field that left-wing thought has never begun to enter. All fiction from the novels in the mushroom libraries downwards is censored in the interests of the ruling class. And boys' fiction above all, the blood-and-thunder stuff which nearly every boy devours at some time or other, is sodden in the worst illusions of 1910. The fact is only unimportant if one believes that what is read in childhood leaves no impression behind.

I believe that what is read in childhood not only leaves an impression behind but also influences the values, and shapes the dreams, of children.

It can provide negative images and stereotypes and cut off hopes and limit aspirations. It can erode self-respect through overt and covert racism or sexism. It can also help young people get beyond family troubles, neighborhood violence, stereotyping and prejudice—all particulars of their lives that they have no control over—and set their imaginations free.

The imagination is usually characterized as the ability of the mind to form images, thoughts, melodies, or equations that are not present to the senses and have not been known or experienced in the past. It is the creative or constructive faculty of the human mind. The imagination gives rise to the idea of possibility, and to the contrast between what is and what might be. The power of the imagination comes from our ability to entertain alternatives to what we have experienced or have been told. The existence of imagination is perhaps the originating force of the ideas of freedom, choice, and the possibility of personal, social, and political change. If we were not able to imagine the world as other than it is, then taking an active role in change would be unthinkable.

Children's imaginations are lively and are fed by the stories they are told and the images provided them by their culture. The role of the imagination in the formation of the self has not been adequately studied. However, in my experience with children I have found that their imaginative responses to stories is not merely imitative. They delight in themes and variations: in, for example, the Little Red Riding Hood tale according to Grimm, and to their own variations of the story, ones that transform the wolf into a weakling and Red Riding Hood into a karate expert, or transform the grandmother into an indigestible poison and the wolf into a corpse. There are many different values manifested in their imaginings—experiments with wickedness, dreams of personal salvation and success, horrid images of monsters, and angelic ones of nurturing figures. The mix of cultural stereotype and personal invention is striking.

However, I believe culture channels the imagination while experience informs it. The imagination responds to hunger in the soul, to longings and pains. And it can be tutored. In our culture the imagination is channeled along personal lines. The stories we provide to youngsters have to do with personal challenge and individual success. They have to do with independence, personal responsibility, and autonomy. The social imagination that encourages thinking about solidarity, cooperation, group struggle, and belonging to a caring group is relegated to minority status. Healthy community life and collective community-wide struggles are absent from children's literature and the stories most children encounter on TV, in film, or at home.

Yet without the encouragement of the social imagination, of freedom to imagine the world being other than it is, we are left without hope for society as a whole. Youngsters who live in poverty and cannot picture a world without poverty are disempowered and as adults easily fall into irretrievable despair. At best they might be able to imagine themselves or their families freed of the pain and trauma of a life of poverty, but the price of personal success is acceptance of the need to abandon friends, relatives, and community. The same holds true for children growing up on murderous streets or living under the weight of racism or sexism. Dreams of personal liberation are important, but moral consistency, self-respect, and healthy communal life imply more than personal liberation. They demand commitment to larger struggles to eliminate victimization.

The dreams and imaginings of oppressed people must embody the shape of a world free of domination if they are to nurture hope. And literature has a crucial role in delineating these dreams and embodying them in stories. The importance of literature in nurturing dreams of freedom has been dramatically illustrated in Czechoslovakia and other parts of Eastern Europe over the past forty years. Novels and poetry, most of it published and disseminated underground, spoke to issues of conscience and human rights. Stories of liberation, fictions of hope contributed to resistance and the eventual overthrow of Soviet domination. Books can be vehicles for sparking utopian and hopeful imaginings. This is as true for children's literature as it is for adult literature. When there are no examples of stories for young people that fundamentally question the world as it is and dream it as it might be, resignation, defiance, or the quest for personal success become the only imaginable options unless the young have other sources for generating hope.

There have been moments in my childhood when my imagination soared and new possibilities for living and acting opened up. These times set me out on paths that have defined the moral quality of my life. For example, I remember when I was about eight or nine sitting around the kitchen table at my grandparents' apartment. It must have been 1945 or '46 and my grandfather's union was out on strike. The strike must have been going on for a while, because the people sitting around the table were on strike and depressed because it was hard to feed their families and keep up their loan payments. One of the men was crying. His wife was sick, they had a new baby, he couldn't pay the heating bill, and he was worried about their ability to survive the strike. Everyone had a sad and wrenching story, and I felt like crying too. I remember my grandfather passing around a bottle of Canadian Club, getting people to pledge help to each other and share what little they had, and then telling them stories about what the world could be like for workers. His stories were told in a mixture of Yiddish and English, and I could only make out their bare outlines. But I knew from the tone and nature of the conversation that they warmed everyone at the table as much as the whiskey did. The storytelling itself inspired me as much as the vision it conjured up of a decent and just future worth struggling for. I think what I got from that evening and many others like it listening to my grandfather was a sense of the power of stories to build comradeship and dedication to social struggle. I learned the importance of imagining good things in hard times, of keeping hope alive and never believing that "reality" was fixed once and for all. Over the years I have learned how to tell stories too, and I've come to realize how important it is for young people to hear tales of justice, to learn of the sorrows and joys of trying to make a better world.

Another moment when the power of the imagination transformed my sense of what the world could be like took place in 1953 when I was a junior at the Bronx High School of Science. I was Bronx Science's representative to the New York City Inter-GO Council, which had two representatives from each of the eighty-six high schools in the city. The council had a weekend retreat in the country for one representative from each of the schools, and I was my school's representative. That weekend was the first time in my life that I spent an extended period of time with people my own age who were not Jewish. I hooked up with a small group of representatives, most of whom were African American and Italian American. After an initial period of finding out about each other, we spent three days and nights sharing our dreams. I remember taking long walks and being part of all-night conversations, forging friendships that lasted for years. The worlds we shared were imagined ones where racism and religious bigotry no longer existed. To my astonishment, across culture, race, and class we had similar dreams and could imagine futures for ourselves and our families that weren't tied to traditional hatreds and fears.

Of course the imagination is not always so benign a power. As much as we have the power to imagine the world better, we also have the power to imagine it worse. In the imagination we can skewer and torture enemies, treat others as objects of our whim, create worlds in which decency is just a rumor. One of the central characteristics of the imagination is that it crosses borders and categories. It is, of itself, neither decent nor indecent, neither good nor evil. It has the power to posit the best and the worst of things and to imagine things beyond moral judgment, such as mathematical theorems, melodies, and machines.

There are other borders that the imagination crosses. It is composed of thought and feeling but is not exclusively either. It is partially driven by the conscious mind and partly by the ruminations of the unconscious. It plays freely but is also determined by what we have experienced. It can be comic or tragic, melodramatic or just silly. It is, in a way, an internal voyager accessible to all people who have not had their minds and spirits destroyed. It makes a person bigger than her or his experience and is the strongest manifestation of the idea of freedom that we know on an intimate level.

From one perspective, the imagination is the power to go beyond experience and, in the mind, to break or change the rules of all the games we are forced to play, whether they are imposed by other people, genetics, or the natural world. It is a source of new rules as well, of thinking the as-yet-unthought-of as we experiment with the development of felt values.

From another perspective, the imagination can be seen as the basis of all experience in the young child. It is out of the spectrum of the possible presented by stories that tease the imagination that the child selects and constructs the "real." The world, looked at in this way, emerges from experiences that inform, shape, and limit the imagination. What is real is negotiated and constructed, and though there is a common core of agreed-upon reality, the rest of our vision of what is real flows through the imagination.

For the sake of both the development of their imaginations and our common future, we owe our children radical stories not only when they are very young but when they are adolescents as well, if only to show them that there are options for collective action to oppose and eliminate oppression and exploitation in all of their manifestations.

For me, a radical story is one that has the following characteristics:

- the major force in the story is the community or some natural social group larger than the family. This could be a neighborhood, a union, a group organized by ethnicity or class. In the story members of the group participate in some collective activity that is centered on an issue of social or economic justice. This could range from a group of girls at a high school organizing to protest sexism to a story about young resistance fighters in Southern Africa or one about Native American youngsters involved in a struggle to keep a toxic dump off tribal land. It could consist of a portrayal of an historical struggle such as the attempt to develop sharecroppers' unions in the South during the 1920s, or of a futuristic battle somewhere in outer space over issues of interplanetary racism and economic exploitation. The range is enormous. What is crucial is that in addition to, or instead of, central plots involving a small number of characters, an overall aspect of the book involves a group working toward unity and focusing on solving a problem of inequity.

- the situation of conflict is one involving a whole community, class, ethnic group, nation, or even the world. Neither love triangles, personal jealousies, struggles over hidden treasure, quests for riches, nor attempts at personal improvement in athletics or health, nor struggles over personally escaping from poverty or oppression would count for me as radical stories. However, all of these could be involved as subplots in the larger story of an attempt to improve the world and create a new order of living.

- collective action is involved, ranging from passive nonviolence to confrontation, and from electoral politics to escape and the establishment of a new community based on principles of equity. In this action the group's survival or dignity and self-respect are at stake, as is its freedom to act democratically. The possibilities range from historical fiction to science fiction, from urban resistance to international struggles for peace, and from stories resulting in major triumphs to those that deal with temporary defeat and the need to continue the struggle in new forms.

- the existence of an enemy who has abused power and who is nevertheless a three-dimensional person or group of people, not an abstract force or mysterious and unknowable entity. Enemies who also live complex lives, have charm and affection, whose lives can be wonderful within the context of family and allies and associates but monstrous when it comes to others are rare if not totally absent in children's literature. In stories about struggles against racism, for example, the focus is often on victims and how they attempt to overcome their victimization. When individuals who are racist are central to the story, they are often portrayed as reluctant victims of ignorance themselves or as people who are good at heart and subject to reform. It is rare if not nonexistent to find an unrepentant racist in children's literature. A similar phenomenon is present in books for young people about overcoming poverty. They do not present the forces that perpetuate poverty or show those people who are responsible for the damage it creates. What makes a book radical for me is its explicit attempt to show opposing forces involved in social struggle. There are people who benefit from the oppression of others, and portraits of such people, in depth and with regard both to their humanity and their responsibility, provide a closer approximation to the circumstances of specific confrontations than does concentration on the victims and their allies.

    Of course, there are many ways in which such opposition can manifest itself and many resolutions to given stories. What makes a book radical is both that it is partisan and that it presents a vision of solutions that are not merely individual but affect entire groups of people. Of course, being radical in this sense does not in itself make a book good or interesting. The question of the quality of radical children's literature is one I'll return to later.

- the story illustrates comradeship as well as friendship and love. It shows the ties of loyalty and unity people develop when they are engaged in a common struggle. This bond can overcome personal animosity, and it can be confused with personal affection. Conflicts within progressive groups are not uncommon, and the tension between the obligations of comradeship and personal matters of the heart often make for dramatic tales within the context of social struggle. In addition, issues of class loyalty versus moral values also arise. I can imagine a book, for example, dealing with struggles to unionize the coal mines in which the mine owner's child joins the miners in struggle against the coal company. There are historical examples of this happening. I can also imagine a book dealing with the Civil Rights movement of the 1960s in which sexism becomes a divisive and central issue among the activists.

• finally, there is no compulsory happy ending or resolution of the problem in radical stories. There are many defeats and regroupings, partial victories, new and larger problems to tackle, and a decent world to sustain or build. What characterizes all the stories, however, is a projection of hope and possibility.

Radical tales should nurture the social imagination and at the same time not be dogmatic or preachy. They have to be personal, intimate, and funny as well as honest about pain and defeat. And if they are all these things there is still no guarantee that they will be good stories. Formulas don't make books, writers do, and what I'm sketching here is a need that exists in children's literature, a hole that exists in the body of work, and not a do-it-yourself kit for radicals.

After years of searching, I've come up with two books that I believe are models of radical children's literature and several more that approximate that form. The two radical books written for young people that moved me, and that my students found exciting reading, were written by the English author Geoffrey Trease. Trease was born in 1909 and raised in Nottingham, and is still writing as far as I know. He attended Oxford for a year and dropped out to work with young people in a settlement house for the poor in the East End of London. He belonged to a radical and somewhat eccentric intellectual circle in London called the Promethean Society, whose major inspirations were Marx, Lenin, Trotsky, Freud, G. B. Shaw, H. G. Wells, Gandhi, and D. H. Lawrence. From this rather strange mixture it's possible to gather that the group combined left-wing politics and an admiration for the newly formed Soviet Union with liberated views on sexuality, and had a tendency toward pacifism. Trease also taught school and set out to change the direction of children's literature by writing about working-class and poor people with dignity and respect. He criticized prior young adult literature as "being rooted in the pre-1914 assumptions which serious adult literature had abandoned . . . [that] the lower orders, like the lesser breeds, figured in only one of two possible roles, as howling mobs or faithful retainers." He had the same concern that Orwell had at the time: that there was no decent, respectful, and compelling writing for young people from a left-wing perspective. It's probably safe to conclude that he had read the Orwell essay quoted above, for he had correspondence with Orwell in 1940 about setting up a left- wing juvenile publishing venture, though the project was never pursued.

In the early 1930s Trease moved from criticizing young people's literature to writing it. For his first book he turned, not surprisingly, to a place and a story he knew from birth: Nottingham Forest and Robin Hood. As he says in the introduction to his radical retelling of the adventures of Robin Hood, *Bows Against the Barons*,

> As a boy in Nottingham, playing with bows and arrows in the park which is still called "the Forest," I always thought of Robin Hood as my favorite hero. But growing up and learning more about life, I felt that some of the stories did not ring true. The "jolly outlaws" could not have found things so jolly, really, and a man like Robin would not have been so ready to fall on his knee before the King. So I tried to create a new picture of Sherwood Forest which should be truer to life.

The tales of Robin Hood date as far back as 1350, and over the years there have been dozens of versions ranging from outlaw tales to tales of politics, religion, and intrigue in the time of the Crusades. A British proverb dating from 1400 went, "Many talk of Robin Hood that never bent his bow," revealing the popularity of the tales as folk knowledge. The most common version of the tales of Robin Hood available in the United States is Howard Pyle's *The Merry Adventures of Robin Hood*. There have also been film versions of the legend, one starring Douglas Fairbanks (in 1922) and another starring Errol Flynn (1938). And Disney, naturally, has produced two cartoon versions of the stories. Knowledge of the stories in the United States might date to before the American Revolution, and reference to them appears in Mark Twain's *Adventures of Tom Sawyer* (1876), where Tom and his friend Joe Harper agree that they "would rather be outlaws a year in Sherwood Forest than President of the United States forever."

The beginning of Pyle's book expresses the tone of the popular versions of Robin Hood that form American audiences' understanding of the legend:

> In merry England in the time of old, when good King Henry ruled the land, there lived within the green glades of Sherwood Forest, near Nottingham town, a famous outlaw whose name was Robin Hood. No archer ever lived that could speed a gray goose shaft with such skill and cunning as his, nor were there ever such yeomen as the seven score merry men that roamed with him through the greenwood shade. Right merrily they dwelt within the depths of Sherwood Forest, suffering neither care nor want, but passing the time in merry games of archery or bouts of cudgel play, living upon the King's venison, washed down with droughts of ale of October brewing.

With four occurrences of "merry," ale, and games, Robin Hood and his band are introduced to the reader as happy and jovial outlaws with no purpose other than to live the good life. Later we are told that they steal from both the king and the undeserving and cruel rich, but their purpose is to feed their merriment. They do, however, have a liberal social conscience and rescue maidens in distress and help the poor:

> Not only Robin himself but all the band were outlaws and dwelt apart from other men, yet they were beloved by the country people round about, for no one ever came to jolly Robin for help in time of need and went away with an empty fist.

"Jolly" Robin has no time for revolution, and one would suppose that there was no need for one in "merry England."

Bows Against the Barons goes against the popular tradition of Robin Hood as represented by Pyle—a good-hearted outlaw, or what Eric Hobsbawm calls a "social bandit" (*Bandits* [New York: Dell, 1969]). In Trease's version Robin Hood becomes a revolutionary leader with a plan for a new socialist England:

> There are no certain facts about Robin in the history books. Yet there is nothing impossible about this tale, even the idea of Robin leading a great rebellion—such a thing actually happened in 1381. In fact, throughout English history many men thought of him as that kind of person. When Walter Raleigh was on trial in 1603, he cried out: "For me, at this time, to make myself a Robin Hood, a

Wat Taylor, a Kett, or a Jack Cade—I was not so mad!" All the
other three men actually led great revolts in England, so Raleigh
must have thought of Robin as a similar leader. (p. 7)

Robin Hood and his Merry Men are a band of guerrillas fighting for
social and economic justice. This could certainly make for a boring and
dogmatic tale, but Trease centers his story on the life of the boy Dickon
who, because of poverty, and in despair, killed one of the King's deer
and fled into Sherwoood Forest. The book begins not with a sermon but
with a drama:

> Crack!
> The long whip curled around his shoulders, burning the flesh
> under his ragged tunic. Dickon swayed sickly, but did not cry out.
> Hi hands tightened on the woolen cap he held, and he bit his lip to
> stiff the pain." (p. 9)

We are immediately plunged into a story that never lets up. In Trease all
of the adventures of Robin Hood are reconceived through the perspective
of conscious social struggle rather than righteous banditry. And since
Dickon, not Robin or his Merry Men, is at the center of all the tales, we
experience Dickon's slow awakening to the larger purposes of Robin, and
to his own commitment to social struggle.

But we also find Dickon, a free agent who has been forced to flee friends
and family, making new friends, getting into trouble, being rescued from
his own mischief. The characters come alive. They are interesting people
whose stories are all variations on a central theme: they were once poor
and subservient people who defied authority and had to flee or be jailed or
killed. They are also intelligent, funny, and skilled, as are the townspeople
and servants in Trease's tales. He admirably achieves his goals of personal-
izing and presenting poor and working-class people with dignity.

At the same time Trease is patient and caring about the landscape. His
knowledge of Nottingham Forest helps him convincingly set the story in a
way that matches the social realism of his approach. He describes the forest that Dickon has escaped to in this way:

> Sherwood was no continuous stretch of dense forest. In places the
> oaks stood well apart, the ground beneath them green with short
> turf and moss. Elsewhere, taller and straighter trees clustered like

silver lances in the moonlight, or clumps of fir and holly presented
thickets too dark and impenetrable for a pathway. Sometimes he
(Dickon) would come on a spacious clearing, carpeted with green
bracken, knee high and more. The scene was always changing . . ."

At the beginning of the tale Trease introduces an ominous note that lets
the reader know that Robin and his men are about serious and dangerous
business. Dickon just barely avoids being detected by a band of the baron's
soldiers, one of whom he overhears saying with evident pleasure, "I could
wish the trees bore more of such fruit." A few pages later Dickon comes
upon a body hanging from a tree, the strange fruit that the soldier had
laughed about.

Trease manages to make his point without having to preach it. Dickon
is educated at the same time that the reader is informed of the fate that
awaits him if he gets caught. The book is intimate, moving, and almost
entirely free of direct preachment. However, during a call to battle, Trease
cannot resist putting his ideas directly into Robin's mouth. Robin
announces to his men that the time for an insurrection has arrived:

> "Some of you are asking: how much longer are we to sulk in the for-
> est, robbed of half of the things that make life worth living? When
> are we going to strike back? My friends, the time grows near. . . .
>
> "We have won the goodwill of the peasants and of the town
> workers. We have proved to both that we are not common cut-
> throats, but their fellow strugglers against the power of barons and
> kings. The time is nearly come for them to join the struggle
> openly—and it is our privilege to lead them. . . .
>
> "All men are equal in the forest," went on the outlaw. "They
> should be equal in the whole world. They should work for them-
> selves and for each other—not for some master set over them. Let
> the ploughman plough for all and the weaver weave for all—but
> let no lord step in to steal the harvest and no merchant prince to
> take the cloth. Then the common people will have twice as much as
> they have now, and there will be no more hunger or poverty in the
> land. . . . There must be an end of serfdom, . . . an end of tolls and
> tithes, and dues and forced services! The land for the peasants and
> the town for the workmen! No more castles, no more hired cut-
> throats in livery, no more war service, no barons, no king!"

The book, which is a delightful read, ends with the cause's defeat and
Robin's death at the hand of the barons and his secret burial by Little John

and Dickon. At the end of Howard Pyle's *The Merry Adventures of Robin Hood*, Richard the Lion Hearted returns to England after participating in the Crusades and assumes the throne. He pardons Robin Hood and his band for their kindnesses to the people. The band disperses and its members fade into middle-class respectability, while Robin himself joins Richard "and he speedily rose in rank to be the chief of all the yeomen." At the very end of his life, he returns to Nottingham, where he defeats the sheriff in battle and then falls sick. He is betrayed by a cousin, a prioress, who, in the guise of leeching him, cuts one of his veins.

In Trease's book Robin is also betrayed, by the prioress after the uprising he has fomented is defeated by the king's forces. Robin is not pardoned, nor is it in his nature to work for royalty. He does not die an old man after retiring as chief of the yeomen. On the contrary, he is wounded in battle and taken to the nunnery for care. He meets his death still a revolutionary with his vision intact. Furthermore, the book does not end with the death of Robin Hood. Since its premise is that collective battles for equity and justice are larger than individual lives, the cause still calls its participants. It does not lose its force with the death of one leader, no matter how central that figure is to the struggle. Thus, Little John says to Dickon just after the death of Robin, referring to their defeat and the disappointment of their ideals:

> "Yes . . . I reckon things will come about slower than we thought. Perhaps not in our time at all. But we'll do our best. Robin was *right*, dead right."
>
> "An England without masters," murmured Dickon, looking toward the hidden grave. "Sounds daft, doesn't it? But he was right. He *dreamed* when the rest of us couldn't see further than our noses."
>
> Little John put a hand on his shoulder. "Shall we go south together, Dickon boy? Back to the High Peak? . . ."
>
> "Right, John. And we'll go on making Robin's dream come true."
>
> Two figures slipped southwards, mere shadows in the wood, their faces set towards the Derbyshire hills."

Young people I have shared Trease's book with identify with Dickon, the sensitive boy trying to make sense of a cruel world without becoming cruel himself. That is the struggle my students face every day. Their lives are hedged in by violence—in the family, on the streets, on TV, and in their dreams. Spaces where hope and struggle are united are very rare in the United States. Yet it is precisely these ruptures of ordinary life, these insights into a way of building a new world while destroying an old and dysfunctional one, that literature like *Bows Against the Barons* provides.

I remember one group of high school students whom I introduced to the book. They were astonished that a story like *Robin Hood* could be set in a way that spoke to their pain and their aspirations. They thought *Robin Hood* was just about a bunch of outlaws who robbed and sometimes shared things with the poor, as members of drug gangs did. They were surprised by the shift in the narrative from what could be called social banditry to revolutionary activity. Of course, they didn't say it exactly that way. What they said was that the only violence they knew happened to them, and they never thought they could use their strengths and the unity inherent in gang loyalty to remake the world. Several of the Latino students, refugees from El Salvador, knew about resistance and spoke up for the first time, telling what it was like to have to retreat to the hills and fight—sometimes to die in the process, or to continue the struggle, and to pray for the future, or go to the United States for refuge and sanctuary.

The release of adolescent passion and intelligence, when validated, can explode into learning. It is a positive force that is too often repressed in schools. Young people who are silent, who sit with their heads down on the desk and pretend to be asleep, can be awakened by literature that speaks to their worries, validates their experience, and offers them a future less horrible than their present. Trease's rendering of fourteenth-century England has such resonance for young people now. In fact, you can love the book without believing any of its politics, though you can't read the book without knowing its politics. That is its brilliance and why I believe that even Orwell would have taken pleasure from it.

Trease wrote another book, *Comrades for the Charter*, which I feel is equally moving and militant. The book, set in 1839, again focuses on young heroes, two boys who have been forced to leave their families because of poverty. They are not unwanted, but there is not enough food to feed them and so they have to fend for themselves. They wander through England in search of bread and, if possible, work. One, Owen, from a Welsh sheepherding community, and the other, Thomas, from an English coal mining community, meet on the road. They are both in search of work and food, not much different from many of the homeless hungry youngsters you can see on the streets of any of our big cities these days. These youngsters are cut away from family and place and have to navigate a world that is most often cruel but sometimes hopeful. However, there is no romance here, for even the hopeful struggles in the book are made against desperate odds and at terrible risk. As the story progresses, the boys become witnesses to, and partisans in, the Chartist movement, but the book is primarily the story of the boys' discovery of meaning in their lives through participating in social struggle.

If you know about the role of the Chartists in the attempt to democratize England, the book can't fail to strike you as an original way to introduce young people to the working-class struggles these people fomented. If you have never heard of the Chartists, the story is still moving.

Owen and Thomas are interesting people, and their struggles are personal as well as political. Their drama carries the reader above and beyond politics, and yet at the same time directly into political struggle. It challenges the reader to consider the value of engagement in struggles with and for others as well as oneself. In the course of the story the author presents a vision of a future in which problems of poverty and exploitation are eliminated. This vision is not realized, but it remains a source of hope and a provocation to the reader. This is the radical component of the text, the dare to dream a better world, one that is fundamentally different from the present one. This is the key to the kind of books Orwell suggested might be written, books that project the possibility of a decent world for all people.

In addition to Trease's books, I have found a small number of other examples of children's books that have many of the characteristics of radical children's literature. A number of them are by Virginia Hamilton. My favorite, and one I believe is a classic, is *The Planet of Junior Brown.* The book is thoroughly different from Trease's work, being neither historical fiction nor the retelling of traditional tales. It is set in contemporary New York, and the best way to describe its genre is social-realistic-fantasy with poetic and biblical resonances. It functions on spiritual, personal, political, and social levels. However, these levels are blended into each other, as what seem to be extended metaphors turn out to be realities, while the characters grow into great dignity and strength and a utopian vision of hope emerges from the depths of homelessness, poverty, and despair.

The strange conjunctions in this book will not be surprising to anyone who is familiar with the extraordinary body of work that Virginia Hamilton has produced. Hamilton was born in Yellow Springs, Ohio, into the Perry family, which had escaped there through the underground railway before the Civil War. During a meeting with her, she told me that her family had preserved traditional stories and understood the spiritual as well as historical worlds of African-descended peoples in America. Her own writing is an extension of this storytelling tradition, and her work ranges from retelling origin tales from all over the world to extraordinary young adult novels that have spiritual depth and a great feeling for the agonies and blessings of growth.

The title character of *The Planet of Junior Brown*, Junior Brown, is African American and a musical genius. He thinks in terms of musical structures: harmonic and contrapuntal relationships. The ebb and flow of emotion in his life is echoed in the same movement in sonatas and concertos. His instrument is the piano, and throughout the book he has to struggle to find one he can use. He also weighs about three hundred pounds and is gentle, lonely, and hungry for friends and social connections. The book begins in a secret basement room in Junior Brown's junior high school. The room is behind a hidden door in a broom closet and contains the workshop of Mr. Pool, the custodian, a former teacher and spiritual guide to Junior and his friend Buddy Clark, who is homeless, streetwise, and as kind as he is angry and likely to explode. The three of them are standing in the dark room illuminated solely by a model of the solar system hanging from the ceiling. It has just been completed and the planets, made of Christmas tree lights, are whirring about in their orbits. There are ten of them. One is the Planet of Junior Brown.

Buddy has put Junior Brown into his solar system. But to draw Junior Brown into his personal world is not as easy. Junior has discovered Miss Lynora Peebs, her grand piano, and her mysterious apartment overflowing with antiques and insinuating a violent life on the verge of chaos. Junior's sad life is retrieved by this piano and Miss Peebs's playing. He lives with his mother and the spirit of his father who, years before when they were living in Mississippi, had walked off, fed up with racism and poverty, and not returned. His mother lives in a fantasy world awaiting the return of her husband, holding tenaciously onto Junior Brown's youth, trying desperately to keep him from growing up and leaving too.

Music is Junior's power. It gives him the ability to turn the world off, to listen to possibility, to create beauty whole out of his imagination. Throughout the book there are moments when it calls him. For example, when talking to Buddy and Mr. Pool, "Behind his eyes, the sound of Miss Lynora Peebs' grand piano swelled in a perfect crescendo as he played it." At other times he can command sound to affect the world. Sitting with his mother at breakfast, he "stops the world" and his mother is "dangled in rhythm with him drinking his coffee. Junior knew the firechord which could make her spin and dance. He played one red tone at a time. Their street crackled, other streets kindled. The city flamed and lived." (p. 108) And when Miss Peebs smashes her grand piano, Junior tells her he can take the lesson sitting on a chair, playing the tune on his lap. The music is within him.

Junior has in him the capacity to inspire and transform the world, but he does not see it. He is too fat, slow moving, sad all the time. Through his connection with Buddy and Buddy's friends he gradually begins to grow independent and at the same time more compassionate and empathetic. He begins to feel with and for others and to understand that his art is of value for others, who are also struggling with problems greater than his own. Junior is not homeless, without family and resources. Buddy, at least on the surface, is.

However, Buddy and the hundreds of other homeless youngsters like him, with the help of some wise adults, remake the world within the midst of a city that feels like it is taken out of *Blade Runner*. This is the radical aspect of the book. There are small utopias dotting the large cruel system. Each of these planets is a collective society of young people aided by wise people like Mr. Pool. They are rebuilding the world from within and resemble small utopian intensive communities.

These poor abandoned young people have created a solar system of dozens of planets, a complex network of compassionate social centers that depend upon kindness and mutual aid. Each planet is a small, democratic collective consisting of youngsters who care for each other, share their earnings and possessions, and try to rescue other young people from despair, racism, and the horrors of enforced criminality. The planets in Mr. Pool's secret room are merely metaphors for the actual planets, the small islands of decency that the rejected have built right within the belly of the beast. Junior Brown, with the help of Buddy and Mr. Pool, is undergoing an apprenticeship so that he too can nurture an actual planet in the basement of an abandoned building or in a loft in a derelict factory building. At the end of the book, Junior is part of the new universe, based on compassion and sharing that is coming into being. The youth indeed shall lead us and save us.

Virginia Hamilton's vision of a city full of planets of the young dedicated to each other's welfare and to remaking the entire planet so that justice will reign is almost prophetic — is moving and memorable. She ends the book with Billy addressing a group he has gathered together to make a planet:

> "We are together," Buddy told them, "because we have to learn to live for each other."
>
> So that was it, he told himself. That was what he had forgotten all these years, or changed with the passage of time to fit with his loneliness. No, his Tomorrow Billy had taught him much more than life as mere survival.
>
> "If you stay here, you each have a voice in what you will do here. But the highest law for us is to live for one another. I can teach you how to do that."
>
> Buddy looked down at Mr. Pool. Their eyes held in a gaze affirming their faith in one another.
>
> Buddy glanced over at Junior. Seeming to sleep, slumped down in the collar of his raincoat, Junior heard Buddy's words in music.
>
> "I'll help you just as long as you need me to. I am Tomorrow Billy . . ." His instinct told him what to do as it always did. Buddy's face glowed with new light. ". . . and . . . this is the planet of Junior Brown."

Though there is no explicit enemy in this book, and the forces that create poverty and disenfranchisement are left remote and mysterious, the central theme of the book is a radical restructuring of personal and social relationships. The book remains silent, however, on the question of confronting existing society and trying to transform it. There is no implication that the planets will spread and overcome the cruel society that has led to their existence. Confrontation with racism and capitalism is not an issue in the book. In that sense I find it utopian rather than radical. This is not meant as a criticism—the book is extraordinary. Nevertheless, it does not exactly fall in the category of radical literature that I find so necessary and so lacking. It points the way, however, and its grounding in the intimate needs of young people for decency and kindness is something to be honored in any attempt to create radical children's literature.

About the same time I first read *The Planet of Junior Brown* I discovered, in Vera Williams's trilogy *A Chair for My Mother*, *Something Special for Me*, and *Music, Music for Everyone* a refreshingly humane, compassionate, and proud world of working people who care about one another. These books, written and illustrated by Williams for primary school children, are profoundly egalitarian, especially the three volumes I heard her once jokingly refer to as her proletarian trilogy. They both confirm and confound my formulas for radical children's literature.

On the one hand, they portray working people with dignity, present an image of collective and compassionate living, and dramatize common struggles to create a decent life. They are unique in primary school literature through their presentation of a complex and loving view of life within a multiracial and multicultural working-class community. This alone is radical in children's literature. However, it is not within the scope of the books to develop a confrontation with the larger society and its social and economic organizations. The books show a community at peace with itself, and there are no social movements that play any role in the stories. Still, they have to be considered by anyone interested in radical children's literature for their focus on the dignity and joy of collective living and daily struggle within a working-class community.

The central figure in all three books is Rosa, a young girl who looks to be about seven or eight. She has brown skin and could be Latino, Jewish, or possibly East Indian, Native American, or African American. It's impossible to stereotype her or her mother and grandmother and yet also impossible to mistake them for middle-class, rich, or White people. Their apartment is sparsely though comfortably furnished and full of photos and other memorabilia, though we are never told anything about their past. Their neighborhood is crowded and street life is abundant. In the illustrations, the people's bodies have the used look that is physical labor's toll. One gets the feeling that the characters all know each other, which is the case in most intact working-class neighborhoods. There is a detailed concrete world portrayed in Vera Williams's paintings that provides the context for Rosa's family dramas and gives the books some of the depth and density of novels. It is that richness of the whole that I find particularly appealing about this trilogy.

A Chair for My Mother, Something Special for Me, and *Music, Music for Everyone* represent what could be called the genre of the commonplace. As both writer and illustrator, Williams skillfully and beautifully portrays ordinary people doing ordinary things. *A Chair for My Mother* is about saving money to buy a comfortable chair, *Something Special for Me* is about choosing the right birthday present, and *Music, Music for Everyone* is about children trying to contribute money to the family and bringing joy to a sick older person. These ordinary events, however, are fraught with the drama that frames working-class existence.

The need for tired, overworked people to save just to afford a comfortable chair is commonplace in the lives of working people who have to struggle to meet their minimal needs. The mother in *A Chair for My Mother* works in the Blue Tile Diner and is on her feet all day, yet the family cannot afford a comfortable chair for her to rest in when she gets home. That single chair is a luxury for the three of them, and understanding their struggle to save enough to buy a chair was a revelation for many of the middle-class children I taught in Berkeley, as moving and distressing as more dramatic losses and needs in fairy tales and adventure stories. Equally important in the story is the closeness of mother, child, and grandmother. They constitute a loving family, and the child's role as nurtured and contributing at the same time is a revelation for children who are either neglected or overindulged. Rosa, the young girl in all three of the books, is rooted in an all-female, loving situation in which the struggle is with economic circumstance and not with each other. That, along with the emphasis on mutual aid, are the elements that make these books feminist, proletarian, and radical. The joy and solidarity they project, along with racial harmony and community cohesion, make them utopian as well.

In *Something Special for Me* the careful selection of just the right birthday present for oneself is an ordinary event heightened by the knowledge that others worked hard and sacrificed their desires to save money for your gift. The present turns out to be an accordion, an instrument I played as a child. I had wanted to play the piano, but the accordion was the closest instrument my parents could afford. Also, the accordion was a pragmatic choice, since playing it well could provide a part-time job playing at weddings and bar mitzvahs.

In the third volume, *Music, Music for Everyone*, learning to work and contribute to the community are presented as components of a decent life. In this finale of the trilogy, Rosa and three friends of hers, all female, two clearly African American and one European American, learn to play instruments and organize a band. The book ends with the band's being paid to perform at a party for one of the band member's great-grandparents. The last page of the trilogy has the four girls sharing what they have earned and Rosa deciding to put her share in the jar where she and her mother and grandmother save money for special things. This is the same jar used in the first volume to save money for a chair for her mother. The story ends where it began, with the economic struggle not merely to survive but to thrive.

It is out of simple, everyday events that Vera Williams, in an understated way, orchestrates words and illustrations and shows how love and mutual respect can bind a family and community together. It is in the particulars of affection that Vera Williams lets her politics show. There is nothing dogmatic about these working-class novels, no preaching to children: just the simple telling of a few tales, whose drama and importance is implicit. They have the character of great literature because they deal with the universals of life that Grace Paley described in her essay *Some Notes on Teaching: Probably Spoken* (from *Writers on Teaching, Teachers on Writing* [New York: Holt, 1970, p. 203]). In the essay, Paley, a friend of Vera Williams who has collaborated with her on a book of poems and paintings, writes,

> It's possible to write about anything in the world, but the slightest story ought to contain the facts of money and blood in order to be interesting to adults. That is—everybody continues on this earth by courtesy of certain economic arrangements; people are rich or poor, make a living or don't have to, are useful to systems or superfluous. And blood—the way people live as families or outside families or in the creation of family, sisters, sons, fathers, the blood ties. Trivial work ignores these two facts and is never comic or tragic.

I'm obviously partial to these books, somewhat because they show the world I grew up in in the way we wanted to be seen, as proud and nurturing.

But it's not the politics or the ethnography of Vera Williams's world that moves the youngsters I've shown the books to. It's the blood and the money, the intimate personal drama and the attractiveness of Rosa, her friends, and her family. The message of the books is that people have to cooperate, share what they have, and pull together if they are to survive with dignity. They represent what my grandfather called working-class pride.

Working-class pride is the opposite of wanting to be rich or to be boss. It is the pride in the power of working people to make a decent world without the help of experts, professionals, or the beneficent rich. This is radicalism from the ground floor, illustrating how democratic socialist ideas play themselves out in everyday lives and, in particular, how they are represented in the actions and dreams of young children.

"All for one and one for all"; "We have to learn to live for each other"; an enormous pickle jar full of change to save for family needs—large visions of a caring and just world are at the heart of radical literature. Geoffrey Trease's early work, *The Planet of Junior Brown*, and Vera Williams's trilogy have tempted me to write a book of my own that Orwell might have recognized as a decent story for young people. But of course wanting to write a book and writing a good book is another thing. Formulas and intentions themselves don't lead to fine literature. However, these three books and other good young adult literature have some components in common that help the process along. Here are some guidelines that I find myself using. They may also be useful for those of you who try to create literature that provides young people with ways of thinking about a world that is fundamentally different—more just and democratic—from the one they experience in their everyday lives and most of the books they read.

In almost all young adult literature, young people are the central actors in the story. They assume powers they often don't have in ordinary life, and they act independent of adult control. Very often this independence is contrived by getting rid of parents or putting parents in situations where they need the help of their children. There are books where the parents are killed off in the first chapter. However, references to parents and family are important, as are the youngster's reflections about their values and the world as they perceive it. Unfortunately, most of these books create small personal or neighborhood worlds for their heroines and heroes and don't make them knowledgeable about larger issues and possibilities. I believe this is characteristic of American publishing, where the paucity of intellectual and artistic life of the young is assumed rather than challenged. It is important to enrich the lives of our young readers by enriching the lives of our young characters as Virgina Hamilton does. Many young people are articulate, thinking, literate, and curious individuals who are justifiably angry at the condescension with which their ideas are treated.

It is not enough to develop thoughtful and interesting young characters without thinking of the setting in which they act and the threats and conflicts that will carry the plot. In a book meant to have a social and political slant, this is a major challenge. The threat cannot be unmanageable—the characters obviously can't all be blown away in the first chapter. Nor can it be trivial. At the same time, there has to be some way in which the characters can contribute to the solution of a problem or at least to a struggle to solve the problem.

A useful device that many authors use is the introduction of a stranger, usually an adult, who offers protection, kindness, and a new vision of how to solve problems and grow up. This adult is not like other adults, but a character whose life allows her or him to have special insight into the inner workings of the human mind or the social world. The role resembles that of a spiritual guide and teacher. It often has classic elements of shamanistic teaching. The shaman is someone who has suffered and fallen from grace, a person of great knowledge gained through complex experience. It is through the process of recovery, often provided by another, elder shaman, that she or he has come to qualify as a teacher and guide of the young. Such characters are often contrasted to formal teachers, whose role is portrayed as didactic and authoritarian rather than indirect and nurturing.

Given a story line with social and moral content that provides a powerful image for rethinking society, one that moves you as a person and a writer, and characters you like (including those from history whose lives are inspiring), a book might emerge. However, as I have been discovering, it is not easy. Since I am urging other people to write radical books for young people and am even presuming to define what that means, it made sense to try to do it myself and answer Orwell in that way. So far I have not succeeded to my satisfaction. However, I thought it would be useful to share the process I've been through, as it might be of use to others who try their hand at creating radical children's literature.

Mother Jones has been an inspirational figure to me for many years. Her guts and her charm, the lilt of her language in *The Autobiography of Mother Jones*, and the sheer courage, trickery, and persistence in her struggles for justice over the 100 years of her life have helped me continue my own work in education with a sense of humor and trickery that tempers the occasional despair that overtakes me.

The section of the autobiography that is particularly inspiring to me is about her children's crusade, which led, in the administration of Teddy Roosevelt, to the earliest Federal Child Labor Laws. Here's a sampler in her own words of what happened:

> The children carried knapsacks on their backs in which was a knife and fork, a tin cup and plate. We took along a wash boiler in which to cook the food on the road. One little fellow had a drum and another had a fife. That was our band. We carried banners that said, "We want more school and less hospitals." "We want time to play." "Prosperity is here. Where is ours? . . ."
>
> I decided to go with the children to see President [Theodore] Roosevelt to ask him to have Congress pass a law prohibiting the exploitation of childhood. I thought that President Roosevelt might see these mill children and compare them with his own little ones who were spending the summer on the seashore at Oyster Bay. I thought, too, out of politeness, we might call on Morgan in Wall Street who owned the mines where many of these children's fathers worked.
>
> The children were very happy, having plenty to eat, taking baths in the brooks and rivers every day. I thought when the strike is over and they go back to the mills, they will never have another holiday like this. All along the line of march the farmers drove out to meet us with wagon loads of fruit and vegetables. Their wives brought the children clothes and money. The interurban trainmen would stop their trains and give us free rides. . . .
>
> We were on the outskirts of New Trenton, New Jersey, cooking our lunch in the wash boiler, when the conductor on the interurban car stopped and told us the police were coming down to notify us that we could not enter the town. There were mills in the town and the mill owners didn't like our coming.
>
> I said, "All right, the police will be just in time for lunch."
>
> Sure enough, the police came and we invited them to dine with

us. They looked at the little gathering of children with their tin plates and cups around the wash boiler. They just smiled and spoke kindly to the children, and said nothing at all about not going into the city.

We went in, held our meeting, and it was the wives of the police who took the little children and cared for them that night, sending them back in the morning with a nice lunch rolled up in paper napkins.

Everywhere we had meetings, showing up with living children, the horrors of child labor.

When I took up Orwell's challenge, Mother Jones became the central character in my thinking. However, I didn't want to write a biography or a fictional account of one of her actual struggles, as Doreen Rapport did in *Trouble at the Mines* (New York: Crowell, 1987). My writing tends to originate with things that worry me. There's a problem that has been troubling me for a while, and until the idea of writing fiction for young people became a challenge I had no idea of how to consider it in my work. I feel sad seeing many young upper-middle-class White children, in particular some of my nephews and nieces, completely disconnected from the struggles against poverty and the social visions of their own grandparents. They look upon their grandparents as outdated, funny old people with ideas that have no moral or spiritual value. And they themselves are struggling to find values without the guidance of the old whom they have rejected and often mock. Their own parents have divorced and they are not part of any community that ranges across age or culture. The are homogeneous unto themselves—a culture of the young and soon-to-be-middle-aged, but with few roots in place or tradition, and hardly any knowledge of family history. I'm caught in the generational middle—loving to be with and understand young people, and beginning to understand the complex stories of my own parents, who are at the end of their lives.

Writing is my way of coming to terms with the unsettling business of being an American. I decided to marry Mother Jones with my concern for White, middle-class children and produce a tale of abandoned children who find themselves in need of older people. I also wanted to show how children of privilege can find ways to use the resources available to them to engage in social struggles. My goal was to have the children I write about become tranformed through meeting with and engaging in working-people's struggles. I used some of what I learned from reading young adult literature. There are three children in the story because I have three chil-

dren, now all in their twenties. They were my models for the children in
the stories. But stories take on identities of their own, and so I decided to
follow the children in their adventure rather than stick to my understanding of Tonia, Erica, and Josh. And I decided, being new to writing young
adult fiction, to make things easier for myself by killing off the parents in
the first chapter. Here's how I began:

I. Running Away

"What are we going to do with them?"

"I don't know. It's so sad and so inconvenient. I don't know
. . . we don't have any space."

"I could probably take one of them for a while but they're really
not my children."

"I wish Mom were alive. She'd know what to do. We had a big
family then and children wouldn't be any trouble. But in Larch-
mont it's so hard to have another person live with you."

"I could take one of the girls; it would be hard but we could do
it. Maybe I shouldn't say this, but I'm angry at Joel and Barbara for
dying, damn it; they've created a problem . . ."

Maxine, Teresa, and Jacob were listening in the next room. They
hadn't recovered from their parents' death and yet were faced with
the terrible problem of where they would live and what they would
do now that there was no home for them. They never particularly
got along with their relatives, but they never fought with them
either. Only now when they thought that the death of their parents
was the biggest problem in the world did they realize that for the living they, too, were a problem — or, more accurately, three problems.

The conversation droned on in the next room as Max, Tessy, and
Jake turned to each other. Anxiety about their future overcame their
grief temporarily. Max, the oldest, spoke her mind as she always did.

"They don't want us and I don't want them either."

Tessy and Jake were more scared than anything else. The children — the whole family — had been very close and the idea of
splitting up was as foreign as the idea of death. Tessy expressed it
clearly: "I'd rather run away than be split up and go to live with any
of them."

"Besides — they don't even want us," Jake added. "We're nothing but a problem to them."

His sisters agreed. They had never felt that they were problems
or burdens before. Max was a bit of a loner, very strong and outspo-
ken, but inner too. She loved to read and sometimes it seemed like
she needed books more than people.

Tessy was quite different. She was a tree climber, a jumper, a wild one who was brilliant and impulsive and in certain ways, fragile. She constantly stretched out and every once in a while fell to pieces in trying to overreach herself.

Jake, too, was one of a kind. There was a temptation to call him a pretty boy. He had blond hair and blue eyes and an engaging smile. Only he didn't use them. They were what he was born with, no more. Beyond the surface he was an analytic, thoughtful, serious person. If he had any major problem it was that he sometimes thought too much when he should have been acting or watching.

Max was 12, Tess 11, and Jake 9. They were faced with a problem that was more serious than anything they had had to deal with before in their lives. Max suggested that they retreat to her room and talk about the possibilities open to them. Nobody noticed them go upstairs—just as no one had noticed that they were listening to the family deliberations over their fate.

And so I had the children run away. They take their savings and go to the 42nd Street bus terminal, traveling by bus down Manhattan from 90th Street and the East Side to 42 St. and the West side, in the course of which they are climbing down the social ladder. When they arrive at the bus terminal they realize that they had merely been running away and had no destination in mind. In a panic they decide to take the first bus to a place they'd never heard of that had a nice-sounding name. Roanoke Rapids, North Carolina, sounded exotic to these youngsters who had spent their lives in Manhattan and Connecticut.

I had friends in Roanoke Rapids who were involved with the textile workers union and part of the struggle to make brown-lung disease qualify for health benefits and worker's compensation as an industrial disease. There were struggles going on that would be foreign to these youngsters, struggles that a modern-day Mother Jones would naturally become involved in. And if such a person existed, surely she would know children in the community; my runaways could easily be hooked up with a family in struggle. So, I landed my three children in the bus terminal in Roanoke Rapids, scared, hungry, and exhausted. They were at the end of the line, with no idea where to go or what to do. However, their resolve not to return to New York and their relatives was still alive:

Before long, they heard that magical name, Roanoke Rapids, and got off the bus.

The bus terminal in Roanoke Rapids could be fitted into a small corner of the one in New York. However, it wasn't the bus terminal that interested Max or Tess or Jake. It was the restaurant and especially the smell of hamburgers. Each of them had two hamburgers, a large order of fries, and two Cokes—which cost $8.50, or about what Jake figured they should spend on food for a day and a half.

They went back into the bus terminal waiting room, full and content. Tess found an empty bench and set her suitcase down. Jake and Max put their knapsacks on top of the suitcase and then the three of them sat down and started waiting. Somehow they expected something to happen to them. They were used to being picked up, driven to lessons or friends' houses, to being taken care of. They thought their adventure would be over when they got to Roanoke Rapids, when in fact it was just beginning.

After a half hour on the bench in the bus station Max began to feel nervous. Tess seemed all right and Jake was almost asleep. But for Max the unreal adventure began to seem all too real. They were in Roanoke Rapids, a strange place, they didn't know anyone there; and they only had $86.50, which no longer seemed like a lot of money. Where would they go and sleep or eat; should they call Uncle Robert? Max tried to look her grown-up best even though she wanted to cry. She was short, strong looking, with a gentle round face that could project imposing strength. She looked around the room. It was almost empty. There was a newsstand, the hamburger shop that they had just left, and a single ticket window, which was closed. There was only one other person in the waiting room, an old woman who looked hard and dirty. She sat in a corner surrounded by bundles, boxes, and shopping bags. Max supposed she was waiting for a bus or for someone to come and pick her up. Her face was almost lost in a shawl she wore about her head. All Max could make out were her eyes, which seemed alternately kindly and harsh. It was hard to avoid looking at her, especially since there was nobody else around, but Max was scared and wished that Tess and Jake could read her mind and tell her what to do about that old lady. She poked Tess and pointed out the woman, who had just gotten up slowly and straightened up her ample and old-fashioned skirt, which was dirty and trailed on the floor. The woman was walking slowly toward them. Tess poked Jake, who woke and looked right into the woman's eyes. Despite himself he tensed and let out a half cry of fear and confusion. The old woman came right to him.

"Don't be scared. This is just how I look. Think of me as your mother. The three of you look like you need some help."

How could they think of her as their mother? Tess felt angry and insulted . . . her mother was young and beautiful, her mother was . . .

"Why are you crying?" The woman's voice had become soft, and her manner was so gentle that Tess went to her and just about fell in her lap crying.

Max tried to be adult. "Forgive her, but we're all tired. We've all been traveling for a long time."

"And where are you going?"

Max hadn't been prepared for that question. Where was she going? She could only be her honest self in answering: "We don't know."

Mother's response was unexpected: "None of us knows, do we, dear? We all know what we have to run away from but finding a place to run to is no easy thing. Why don't the three of you come with me and I'll find a place for you to sleep and some children for you to play with."

Max, Tess, and Jake looked at each other. Could they go with a stranger? They were always told not to trust people. But they were also told that their lives would never change, that if they did well in school everything else would be taken care of, that they would never have to make decisions like this one that might change their lives or hurt them. They looked at each other, and more out of a lack of any other thing to do in Roanoke Rapids than their own resolution and strength, they decided to go along with this woman, who suggested that they think of her as their mother.

The children find themselves settled in a home with other children and are drawn into a life completely different from the one they knew. They also discover a warmth and community that was unknown to them, and an omnipresence of pain and hunger that astonishes them. Mother tries to soothe their way as they learn how to listen to others and think less about their petty concerns. There is a fundamental decency in all three children, and they try to make moral sense of the contrast between the world they have thrust themselves into and the world they grew up in. Fortunately they have Mother's help. She takes them to the modest home of a family who are friends of hers. The mother and father work at a textile mill.

The children make friends through the children in the family and are drawn into many unfamiliar (to them) aspects of life in a working-class family. The family is involved in union struggles, and a strike is about to begin.

The whole dynamic of working-class struggles is new to them, and somewhat overwhelming. They have learned to be comfortable living with their hosts and have made friendships, but the continual hardship of it all is wearing them down just as it has done to all the people in Roanoke Rapids that they have come to love. Mother tries to bring them along and shows them ways they can help in the family and community's struggles. She also fills them in on some history and shares the people's stories with them:

> Tess was just about out of breath when she and Mother arrived at Michael's Print Shop. She had been trying to keep up with Mother as she walked though streets and alleys and across roads talking all the time, trying to find out about Tess and tell Tess something about herself. Tess tried to figure out what Mother was talking about. She said something about once having had a family, about not having one place to live but living in many places with many people who were as nice as Alice Jeanne, and about seeing where people worked and whether they liked their work. It was all new and strange and Tess had an even harder time describing her life and her parents to Mother, who asked her what her parents did. She said her mother mostly stayed home but sometimes she went to meetings where people talked about ways to help poor people and retarded children. It was hard to talk about her mother, who she could still see whenever she thought about her. It was even harder talking about her father because all she knew was that he went to work. She didn't know what he did other than make money so they could all have things to eat and live in a nice place and go to good schools. Mother never pressed her either, and when she saw that walking and talking and remembering was causing Tess pain, Mother insisted they stop and have a soda. Mother was angry with herself, too. She had asked too much, wanted to teach too fast.
>
> They arrived at Michael's. Tess was weary and Mother looked troubled. Michael changed all of that. As they walked in the door he ran to them.
>
> "There's an emergency. Thank God you're here. What would I do without you?"
>
> It was hard to believe a word of his, considering his smile and confident and loving presence. He did have a problem though. He saw Mother's face and couldn't bear to see her unhappy, and knew that what made Mother happy was helping other people with their problems. Michael was a master of thinking on his feet. He made up something for Mother to solve.
>
> "I have this folder to get out for a Brown Lung meeting tonight,

and we have everything but the headline. What can we say in one line to get people to come? Mother, you have any ideas?"

Mother forgot everything but Brown Lung and the fact that she was still needed for someone's struggle. She thought of the empty line at the top of the page and played with short tough phrases: Leave the Mills and Die; Sleep on the Sheets You Made; Peace in a Lint Free World; The Fabric of Death . . . none of the titles was right and Mother felt tired and uninspired.

Tess was troubled by the question and asked what seemed to her a very simple question: "Are there really people who have brown lungs and what's so bad about that anyway?"

Michael and Mother, who would usually have jumped on anyone who asked such a naive question, looked very closely at Tess and saw that she was puzzled, not hostile. She didn't know. She wanted to learn. Their lives had been so consumed by the struggle to help people who were dying from Brown Lung disease as well as others who were working in the mills that they usually had no tolerance for people who simply didn't know what they were so bothered about. But Tess was different. Mother liked her and suspected she would end up loving her. And Michael knew that Tess was important to Mother even though he had no idea why. Because of their special concern for Tess, they didn't get angry at her for her ignorance of their struggles and gently tried to explain to her what the problem was. Mother chose her words carefully.

"You see, textile mills are where sheets and towels and pants and shirts are made. In those mills there are a lot of people who work for very little money and sometimes they have to do jobs that hurt them. There are people who work around lint all the time and breathe in so much of it that it ruins their lungs, and then they can't work anymore and are too poor even to get the right kind of medical care . . ."

Tess was puzzled: "You mean the fuzz my mother used to brush off our sheets and clothes can hurt you?"

Michael tried to explain: "If you stand in a pile of lint all day so that it sticks to your clothes and gets all over your skin and is in the air all the time, it can hurt you. Not at home though. Some people at the mills are so covered with lint during the day that they look like they're made of balls of cotton."

That seemed funny to Tess, though she knew it was a serious matter for Michael and Mother and summoned her most serious adult-sounding voice and said: "Well, I think it's wonderful that you're doing something to help those poor people." She felt embarrassed after she said that though, for she realized that she sounded just like her mother's friends, who always ran around working for a good cause and who her father used to call "those silly do-gooders" . . . and she also wondered why anyone would be so stupid to work in a mill anyway if the work was so hard and you could get sick.

Mother replied, almost angrily, "We're working with them so that they can help themselves," and then turned back to her task, upset with herself for getting upset at Tess. She knew Tess didn't know anything about poor people or the work they had to do and resolved to be patient and let her find out things for herself. Mother was a magician at helping people discover strengths they never knew they had, only with Tess it was different; Mother felt an urgency about teaching the children everything she knew that was new to them. Were they like the children she lost years ago in that fire? Would she hurt them and herself by caring too much about these three strangers?

After a while they decided upon a headline: THE SECRET IS OUT: COTTON DUST KILLS. Michael went right to the back room and in ten minutes emerged with three bundles of material printed for the Brown Lung meeting. Mother took two and Tess took one, and they left. The way home seemed endless to Tess. She was tired and wanted to see her brother and sister and find a place to lay down and read or listen to music or even stare at the wall in silence.

I haven't been able to go on from here. My idea is to have the children return to New York at some time and find a way, in their middle-class world, to deal with the same problems that they come to understand in Appalachia. The last thing I want to do in the story is have the children be rescuers of people hurting more than they are. On the contrary, I want them to become committed to confronting the world that causes or tolerates such poverty and oppression and at the same time be friends for life with the people in Appalachia who have been so kind to them.

At the moment of writing this I have reached what might be called "the Orwell limit." I don't want to preach, I need the story to be organic, and I am currently out of ideas on how to put it all together. I feel that the children I've created are tired and want to go home. The tension between what they are telling me they want to do and the way I want the story to go is irresolvable for me at the moment. It may be that in the future I'll be able to understand what needs to happen in the story and finish it. It may also be that having come this far, I've learned all I can from this particular attempt and need to begin again. I look on an attempt like this not as a failure but as a learning experience that has given me the opportunity to stretch out into writing juvenile fiction and explore the relationship among values, plot, and character.

The need for radical children's literature has never been so great. School, TV, and casual conversation at home and on the streets are all silent on decency. There has never been a period in my lifetime when it has been so urgent for children to know that there is more than one way to organize society, and understand that caring and cooperation are not secondary values or signs of weakness so much as affirmations of hope and life. I urge people to try their hand at creating this new literature for young people, keeping in mind that, as Orwell reminded us, radical vision must be informed by a deep humanity that has a high regard for the individual as well as the society. I see this literature as a gift to our children, a way of helping them nurture their dreams and keep their imaginations alive.

And, I tell myself, if *Mother and the Children* doesn't work out, there's always Christopher Snider.

WICKED BOYS AND GOOD SCHOOLS:
THREE TAKES ON PINOCCHIO

A Note to the Reader: These three essays can be read as themes and variations on the role of stories in education. The first essay focuses on Carlo Collodi's *Pinocchio* and deals with the development of literacy. The second shifts to Angelo Patri's *Pinocchio in America* and is concerned with learning how to question. It is also an introduction to the great Italian American progressive educator Angelo Patri and leads directly to the third essay, which considers the educational work of Patri and his friend and colleague, Leonard Covello. This last essay concerns the role of stories in the education, development, and preservation of community.

TAKE 1: READING *PINOCCHIO*

Children can learn the fundamentals of critical reading before they learn the alphabet. There is a natural and continuous relationship between listening and speaking on the one hand and reading and writing on the other. Children as young as four and five can listen to complex stories and question them—learn to speculate about the author's intent, hidden meanings in the text, and the social and cultural background of the work. They can learn to think clearly and speak well as they learn to read. After that the development of reading skills per se is not a big deal. Once children understand the riches in written texts and want access to them, mastery of the mechanics of reading requires little more than patience and a supportive reader, adult or child, to answer simple questions about sounds and meanings. What is key to set children on the route to literacy is a few good stories and an adult or another child who likes to talk about tales. Content and conversation are the essential components of literate thought. The development of intelligence and sensitivity emerges through the challenges of stories. And *Pinocchio* is a challenging story, one that bears critical reading in the kindergarten.

When I was teaching kindergarten and first grade, *Pinocchio* was one of my students' favorite stories. They loved the rogue and delighted in his mischievous ways. They were not chastened when he was turned into a donkey, and they didn't learn from Pinocchio's other mishaps that the unbridled quest for joy leads to unhappiness. They were sympathetic when he sold his schoolbook for a ticket to a puppet show and cheered him on during his career in the theater. Throughout all his sufferings, they were confident that he was brazen and clever enough to escape, and they turned the usual reading of the tale on its head by taking his sufferings not as the wages of sin but as the trials that had to be born for the fun he experienced.

The one event in Pinocchio's life that they did not like and that jaded his otherwise attractively wicked career was his first encounter with Talking Cricket, the Jiminy Cricket of Disney fame. Talking Cricket had lived in Gepetto's house for over a hundred years, and he tried to give Pinocchio the wisdom of those years. He advised the puppet to give up his errant ways and go to school or at least learn a trade. In the middle of his sermon, Pinocchio picked up a mallet and threw it, hitting the cricket and leaving him "dried up and flattened against the wall." (p. 19) As we talked about the story, many of the children kept on returning to this action—"How could he do such a thing?" and "Can you like a character if they show that they can be so cruel?" This last was particularly vexing for some children, who found themselves drawn to Pinocchio and fearing him at the same time.

The Pinocchio I introduced to my students was not derived from the Walt Disney movie nor any of its children's book spinoffs but came directly from a wonderful translation of Carlo Collodi's Italian original, which first appeared as a newspaper serial in 1881 (*The Pinocchio of C. Collodi,* trans. by James T. Teahan [New York: Schocken Books, 1985]). Collodi (a pseudonym for Carlo Lorenzino, b. Nov. 24, 1826, in Florence; d. Oct 26, 1890) took part in the *risorgimento,* Italy's struggle for unification and independence from French and Austrian domination, and he wrote satirical columns for a newspaper he founded. In 1875 he decided to write for children "because grown-ups are too hard to satisfy."

Pinocchio according to Collodi is not the same as Pinocchio according to Disney. The most striking difference is that Collodi's Pinocchio never becomes a good boy and is not even expected to become a model of obedience and conformity. That's why he is such a compelling figure for my students. Pinocchio is and remains mischievous—he's always testing the limits and willing to take chances. He's not the innocent victim led astray, as Disney portrays him, but a troublemaker whose mischief often rebounds against him. Even before he becomes a puppet—when he is a spirit locked inside a piece of wood—he causes trouble. In the second chapter of the book Gepetto, the puppet maker, gets kicked by Pinocchio while Pinocchio is still a stick of wood. Even while the puppet is being carved it causes trouble. When Gepetto carves Pinocchio's eyes they roll over and stare brazenly at Gepetto. When the nose is carved it keeps on growing no matter how much Gepetto tries to cut it down. When the mouth is carved the puppet laughs and sticks its tongue out. When a hand is carved it snatches Gepetto's wig. And when Gepetto makes feet Pinocchio instantly runs away. It takes a member of the carabinieri to run him down and return him to Gepetto. There is not even a moment of commerce between Pinocchio and his liberator, not a nod of appreciation, much less a thank-you. When told well, this scene is hilarious, but not without overtones of menace and mystery. Pinocchio is a spirit released from a piece of wood, and children don't forget that as they listen to his adventures. There is something magical about him from the very start. Disney invests Pinocchio with an innocence that is wholly lacking in the original.

During his adventures Pinocchio encounters a "beautiful child with blue hair" who turns out to be his guardian angel. Her advice is routinely ignored. But two incidents in the story cause Pinocchio to become a real boy instead of just a puppet. When Gepetto gets sick Pinocchio works hard to take care of him, and when he hears that the Blue Fairy is ill he also helps her. It is these acts of family generosity and loyalty that redeem him. As the Blue Fairy says at the end of Collodi's book:

> Pinocchio. . . . To reward you for your good heart I will forgive you for all that is past. Boys who minister tenderly to their parents and assist them in their misery and infirmities are deserving of great praise and affection, even if they cannot be cited as examples of obedience and good behavior. Try to do better in the future and you will be happy.

The book *Pinocchio* does not preach unmitigated virtue. Pinocchio does not become the perfect child and good boy that Disney projects at the end of the film; boys will be mischievous, now and forever, and perhaps that's a good thing as long as they learn to care for other people and try to be good. Wickedness is part of nature: Pinocchio's desire to run away and make more mischief is never conquered.

Because of the moral ambivalence of *Pinocchio* it is a wonderful story for children. It provokes questions about good and evil, temptation, responsibility, and the calls of family loyalty. I've discussed the work with five- and six-year-olds, and, using the story as a way of focusing the conversation, we've been able to have dialogues on these complex metaphysical and ethical questions. Since the goal is to read and appreciate the tale and not make moral judgments about the children's behavior, our talks do not have to be tied up neatly. There's no need to draw final conclusions, write down homilies for the children to parrot, or even come down on the side of good or evil. The intent of discussing the text is to get greater pleasure and understanding from the story.

Still, it is important to express some concerns about Pinocchio as a role model for boys. The implication is that boys and men are mischievous, full of adventure, apt to get into trouble, but ultimately redeemed through their ability to help when help is needed. This implies a tolerance for male mischief or at least an acceptance of it as inevitable. In real life the victims of this mischief, however, are too often females, and to accept this is to consign women to the role of patient witnesses of their own oppression. "Boys will be boys!" is a very dangerous attitude, one that leaves the door open for the sanction of male violence.

The passive role of women and old folk is reinforced by Pinocchio's nurturing role in the story. Gepetto and the Blue Fairy are dependent on him; they are both victims of his mischief and beneficiaries of his grace. He often ignores their good advice, but at bottom his heart is with them, and he has the power to rescue them.

One could also surmise from the book that girls are expected to be the opposite of boys, if only by their complete exclusion from Toyland and all of Pinocchio's other adventures. Girls are not even tempted by the Fox and the Cat and the other rogues that Pinocchio encounters. They are denied the pleasures of sin as well as saved from the punishments. And despite their delight with Pinocchio, the troublemaker, my kindergarten and first-grade students clearly saw the sexism in the story when we read the book. In the critical context of our reading and talking about the text, the sexism inherent in *Pinocchio* could be integrated into our appreciation of it. In a way this was preparation for the children to read the canon later in their educational careers, and know how to manage texts like *Ulysses, The Golden Bowl,* and *The Great Gatsby,* in which they would surely discover sexism, racism, and classism. My idea was to set the groundwork for their ability to critique texts, understand the biases and deficiencies in some books, and still be able to appreciate and enjoy their brilliance and wisdom.

The girls in my kindergarten had a working knowledge of mischievous boys in the class and didn't like being their victims. In fact, one of the explicit problems I had to work on was what could be called the habits of mischief that many of the boys had been rewarded for at home and on the playground. Some of their parents felt that boys' making mischief was cute and functional—a sign of their ability to be aggressive and competitive in the future. Annoying and dysfunctional boy behavior was tolerated because its adult manifestations were thought to be functional in the business and professional worlds.

For me mischief was a delight when it served to question arbitrary rules or test out a situation without hurting or insulting anybody. I like some aspects of Piniocchio's irreverence myself, and one of the reasons I chose to read the book with the class was to create an occasion for the discussion of the limits of mischief and the development of empathy. Stories, delightful in themselves, are also powerful vehicles for the discussion of sensitive issues in a nonemergency situation. When there is an immediate abuse to deal with in the classroom—a case of one child picking on another or ostracizing her or stealing from him—then that particular instance has to be dealt with directly. It is foolish to try to generalize, tell a story, or preach or bring everyone together and have a class discussion: There is too much self-esteem at stake on the part of all the children involved, both those who were abused and their abusers. In situations like this my goal as an educator is to provide comfort and justice for the hurt children and limits and counsel for the ones who choose to damage others. I try to get beyond instances of abuse as well and as quickly as possible, but I don't forget the larger moral issues involved. Stories become tools to approach and investigate these issues with students. They provide problems at a distance, moral dilemmas to discuss and examine, rather than conflict situations to be resolved.

I choose my stories very carefully, sometimes deliberately to provoke dissent and disagreement, though I hope always to charm or challenge. Though I have no idea how the discussion will go when I use *Pinocchio*, it is clear that certain issues will arise. *Pinocchio*, for example, raises the issue of boys' mischief, the role of girls in the world of adventure and trouble-making, and loyalty to family. Therefore it was no surprise that the issue of sexism in the story was brought up by one of the girls. Her question went something like this: "How come people let boys tease you and think it's cute and if a girl does it to boys they say girls should be polite?"

We had a lively conversation on mischief, with a few of the boys defending their rights to harass others if they were strong enough to get away with it. They even upped the stakes and indicated that they would rather be the evil Fox or Cat or the Ringmaster than Pinocchio. I raised the issue of the problem of the tables turning and tricking the trickster, and we talked about people always meeting someone stronger than they are. One of the students commented that Gepetto probably was really stronger when he was young but that getting old makes everyone weaker and more dependent.

The boys reluctantly agreed that they wouldn't be strong forever, and we moved to the question of whether being a boy was any different from being a girl. However, some of the boys, like Pinocchio, didn't remember their own words, and their mischief, though abated, was a continual challenge throughout the school year.

It may sound surprising that conversations of this level of sophistication occurred in a kindergarten/first-grade class, but that is only because they are not often solicited. These same students, for example, rebelled when I administered the California Test of Basic Skills. There was a question, accompanied by a picture of a woman mopping a floor, that went something like this:

She likes to: a—map. b—pop. c—mop. d—hop.

One of the girls in the class raised her hand and called me over and pointed to the question. I asked what was wrong and she said that the woman didn't "like" to mop so she wouldn't answer the question. Natu-

rally all the other students heard the conversation and agreed. I was pan-
icked because the test was timed, and I told them to skip the question and
get on with the test. Later on we discussed the question and agreed that
the test maker was making a sexist assumption. I also filled in the correct
answer on all of the children's answer forms as they certainly knew the
"correct" answer and were right in not providing it.

Just as we were finishing *Pinocchio* a girl in the class raised a very important question. We had discussed the sexism in the book, the problem of
boys' mischief, and the way in which adults just wouldn't let Pinocchio be
but were always preaching to him. Some of the discussion was very hard
on Collodi, since some of the students fell into the graduate school
dilemma of critiquing details in the text while losing the magic of the
whole. The question we had to work through was: Even if there are things
wrong with the book, can we still like it?

That same question can be asked of *Huckleberry Finn*, *The Heart of
Darkness*, and many other books whose content is shaped by stereotypes
that the author accepts and prejudices the author manifests. Can a reader
like a book that is offensive on ideological grounds? Should children be
put in situations where they are required to read such books or participate
in their being read and discussed?

My response in class was to ask my student whether in fact she did like
the book. She said she did, even though there were some things about it
she didn't like. In particular, she liked Pinocchio and said he was kind of
like her, always acting without thinking but really very kind. In that case, I
told her, like it away and don't ever let anyone take your liking away from
you. As long as you can think about the problems with a book, understand
its imperfections, and still like it, don't let public pressure steal the authen-
ticity of your feelings. And, I also commented, if she decided she didn't
like it even though it was a "classic," she had that right too.

There are books that are wonderful though offensive. I can like Celine
or read T. S. Eliot with pleasure and still find their politics offensive. I don't
like the attitude that someone else can judge the content of a book for me,
and I don't prejudge books for my students. I do, however, insist that we
look at what is read from a critical point of view and weigh the multiple
components that shape personal responses to complex works of literature.

There is some literature that offends me so deeply that I cannot like or even manage to finish it. Once I read C. G. Jung's writings and found his ideas compelling. However, after having worked my way through about eight volumes of the collected works, I came upon an essay on a brief visit he made to Africa. In the essay he described the dances and rituals he had observed as manifestations of the savage, primitive, pre-intelligent phase of humanity's development. The arrogant tone of his voice and the ignorance and racism he displayed repulsed me and caused me to reinterpret everything of his I had read and admired before. From that day on I have been unable to read Jung with pleasure and have only looked at his work when required to for the sake of quotation or criticism. I take this as a visceral personal response and not a universal judgment on the quality of Jung's work or his pyschological contributions.

In a similar way, after reading Chinua Achebe's essay "An Image of Africa: Racism in Conrad's *Heart of Darkness*" (from *Hopes and Impediments*) I tried to reread Conrad's book and found myself repulsed. When I first read it over twenty years ago I was drawn into the tale and gained insights into my own fears by giving myself up to Conrad's tale. Through reading Achebe, the text has been transformed and gives me no pleasure or insight into anything beyond the pervasiveness of racism in this work of Conrad. As Achebe says at the end of his essay:

> Conrad saw and condemned the evil of imperial exploitation but was strangely unaware of the racism on which it sharpened its iron tooth. But the victims of racist slander who for centuries have had to live with the inhumanity it makes them heir to have always known better than any casual visitor, even when he comes loaded with the gifts of a Conrad. (p. 20)

This new awareness of the text has diminished the pleasure and insight I originally gained from the story and led me to devalue it. Such devaluation of the so-called classics is a potential result of questioning a text, of examining its biases and its relationships to issues and struggles in your own life. And different people will come away with differing relationships to an examined text. I find this reevaluation healthy, even in situations where the text is as simple as *Pinocchio* and the reader is five or six.

It took about two weeks in my kindergarten/first-grade class to read and discuss *Pinocchio*. It also took a good chunk of time each day. We could go on for as long as two hours on rare occasions, and our usual hour hardly ever seemed like enough time to read and discuss the work. Our daily reading sessions were always accompanied by discussions in which we speculated on the text and critiqued it. The children learned how to, as Paulo Freire puts it, "question the text." By questioning the text the children were encouraged to propose different versions of the story, imagine what the author had in mind, and think about the effect of the book upon themselves not merely as readers but also as males and females and as African Americans and European Americans experiencing the same text in different ways. Because the class read many different types of books throughout the year, and because the reading was accompanied by questioning, probing, rethinking, and critiquing the text, I had no problem choosing a book that, though it was a classic and delightful in many ways, had sexist components. I wanted the children to critique and reflect upon *Pinocchio* since I knew they would encounter him by way of Disney as part of their culture, and I believed that it was useful for them to experience a critical take on a common text.

Literacy, the intelligent and imaginative understanding of texts and experiences, is at the center of decent education. Reading out loud and open-ended discussion, starting from the text and reaching into the students' lives, is at the heart of my teaching and has been for over thirty years, whether I'm teaching adult education, graduate school, high school, fifth grade or first grade, reading Sartre or Superman. Just last summer a graduate class I taught at Simon Fraser University in Vancouver read, out loud and with continual and often very personal conversation, Lisa Delpit's article "The Silenced Dialog" in exactly the same way as my kindergartners and first-graders read *Pinocchio*. The ability to listen to a story (either aurally or through signs) and to speak intelligently about it is at the center of the development of intelligence and the active imagination.

Literacy, though personal, develops socially. It is not an individual matter, as most educators would have it. Within circles of learners, often with a more experienced teacher, but also within a circle of peers, the ability to question and examine an issue, thought, idea, or feeling arises most naturally. It is also where the habits of sensitive reading and studying develop.

There are certain agreements that make circles of learning possible, and these agreements hold equally across age and subject matter. First of all, there is no grading whatever within a circle of learners. All response is voluntary, and whenever people go around a circle and are asked to respond, each member of the group has the right to pass without being evaluated. This means that a member of the group can remain silent throughout the entire process as long as he or she agrees to listen. Listening holds a high place of honor in the group.

In addition, as long as the central theme or text remains the focus of the group, members are encouraged to contribute stories and personal experiences, and to put questions to the group leader or anyone else in the group. They are not, however, allowed to change the subject totally, deliver a speech on their own agenda, or disrupt anyone who is contributing.

I began to explore this kind of group learning with my whole class at the very beginning of my teaching career. There was no theory behind it. My main impulse was to find a way for the class to speak together about interesting and important things and get caught up in ideas. There was no space for this kind of discussion in the curriculum, where everything was a matter of preplanned question and answer. The intellectual and personal wandering and dialogue characteristic of good and thoughtful conversation were missing from the curriculum. On the other hand, stories and the thoughts they provoked were a vehicle to the development of an intellectual community in the classroom—even more than that, they were manifestations of such a community.

In that community the teacher has a difficult and central role, and this kind of work within a group should never be mistaken for letting everyone do their own thing or say whatever they want. It is focused, and the teacher's job is to find texts, read or set up group readings, raise initial questions, challenge, prod, joke, provoke, but never grade. Reward and punishment, reinforcement, or any of the trappings of behavioral manipulation have no place here.

So reading *Pinocchio* wasn't just reading *Pinocchio*. It was my way of introducing my students to the life of the mind, the value of their own experience and stories, and the courage to raise interesting and challenging questions. It was also introducing them, in a social context, to reading as dialogue with a text, as an act in which their own experience is important and their own mind active. At the same time it was introducing them to studying a text and being able to communicate about ideas. It was about helping them learn how to value their own and other people's voices. And finally it was a step, within a supportive group, toward helping them internalize the group process and become active intellectuals in their own right.

The Brazilian educator Paulo Freire, author of *Pedagogy of the Oppressed*, wrote a short essay titled "The Act of Study," in which he eloquently elaborates on some of the aspects of learning that I have discovered independently through my practice over the years. Freire, however, refers to a mature personal practice, one that I see beginning with social practice in childhood and becoming internalized over time.

For Freire,

> The act of study . . . is an attitude toward the world. Because the act of study is an attitude toward the world, the act of study cannot be reduced to the relationship of reader to book or reader to text. In fact, a book reflects its author's confrontation with the world. It expresses this confrontation. And even when an author pays no attention to concrete reality, he or she will be expressing his or her own special way of confronting it. Studying is, above all, thinking about experience, and thinking about experience is the best way to think accurately. One who studies should never stop being curious about other people and reality. There are those who ask, those who try to find answers, and those who keep on searching. Maintaining this curious attitude helps us to be skillful and to profit from our curiosity. In this way we use what we have already learned in confronting everyday experience and conversation.

Thus our reading of *Pinocchio*, discussing him and our own lives and taking pleasure in the text at the same time as taking pains with it, was an introduction to studying the word and studying the world. It was a small way of helping my students gain some personal power while at the same time learning the pleasures of study and communication within a group. For a teacher, the ability to plan and participate in, as well as learn from, these circles is one of the greatest joys of teaching. It is to participate in a great play of the imagination where, once again in the words of Freire, "To study is not to consume ideas, but to create and re-create them."

TAKE 2: ANGELO PATRI'S *PINOCCHIO IN AMERICA*

So what happened to Pinocchio after he returned to Gepetto at the end of the book? Did he become a boy and go to school and settle down? Or did he, at the last moment, get wanderlust again and take off on new adventures? It certainly wouldn't be surprising if an Italian youth of Pinocchio's age and time decided to join tens of thousands of compatriots and run away to America. And Angelo Patri, one of the pioneers of progressive education in the New York City school system, and an immigrant who arrived in New York City from Italy as a child around the turn of the century, does take Pinocchio to New York in his long-out-of-print book *Pinocchio in America* (Garden City, NY: Doubleday, Doran, 1928). Patri's Pinocchio is a marionette, an untransformed and unrepentant troublemaker who wants things the easy way.

In the introduction to the book Pinocchio himself tells us, "I'll go to America where children are free" (p. xiv) and then turns his narrative over to Angelo Patri, whose tale begins with Pinocchio's return to Gepetto from adventures in Africa.

The patient Gepetto welcomes Pinocchio home and prepares him, for the hundredth time, to go to school like a good boy. Pinocchio even gets as far as spending one whole day in class where, he falls asleep and dreams. In his dream a star appears and calls to him, "Pinocchio, I am your star. Rise, follow me to the Western world where lies your fame and fortune. Rise and follow me." (p. 6) Upon awakening Pinocchio heads to the sea without even bothering to say good-bye to Gepetto and swims through the Mediterranean and across the Atlantic Ocean. He arrives in the New World without sword or hat, his gleaming paint worn down to a "sad gray-green," just like an immigrant, and is washed up on shore somewhere in New York. His first words in America are addressed to Christopher Columbus, to whom he pleads:

> "Sweet Christopher Columbus, come to my aid. Did I not swim where you sailed? Did I not, like you, follow my star to the Western world? Are we not brothers in adventure? You would not forsake a little brother? You would not let me suffer for a few brushfuls of paint and a willing hand to lay them?" (p. 12.)

Pinocchio's prayer is answered. He is mistaken for driftwood by two young children who take him home for firewood.

Patri confronts Pinocchio with his great menace, school, in the first half of the book. The mother of the children who found him on the beach happens to be Italian and recognizes the great and famous Pinocchio. She repaints him and makes him a hat and sword. Newly refurbished, he is sent to school and duly runs away, seeking not learning but fame and fortune.

After a series of misadventures Pinocchio is grabbed by social services and confined to a school for wayward boys, where he is required to repeat that 2+2 equals 4, which he refuses to do. Ever resistant and independent, he insists that 2+2 is "enough," not 4. He is confined to a room where a great big rooster pecks at his head and slaps him with its wings, asking over and over, "How many are two and two?" Finally Pinocchio gives up and says, "Tell me, Excellency, and I shall know." To which the rooster replies, "No use telling you. First place you wouldn't believe it. Second, you wouldn't remember it. Third and forever, it wouldn't be the right answer for you because the right answer for me is the wrong answer for you, although the answer always comes to four. . . . You've got to work. You've got to work. You have to find your own four. Why don't you look in your book." (pp. 76–77)

Worn down, Pinocchio looks in his book and sees not 2+2 but the lovely Blue Fairy and sad Gepetto waiting for him at home in Italy; sees himself running and running and always alone and friendless and hungry and sad. The Blue Fairy then helps him with this advice: "You must be your own friend and help yourself. Two and two are always four, Pinocchio. Remember that. No matter how you try to change the answer, it always comes back to four. Try to remember, and by and by you will understand, if you will only try to look behind things. Look behind books, behind words, behind actions. Search."

And Pinocchio duly says four when asked the next time, and he is rewarded. But, of course, "Not one word of what the fairy said, or of what the teacher meant, or of what the Watchful Rooster had pecked into him did that little woodenhead understand." (p. 80) In fact, the next night he manages to run away from school again for a day. But there is no escape. He returns to school defeated and is watched over by the Rooster as his lessons are forced upon him. Still, no matter how pecked, harassed, and harangued he is, nothing seems to penetrate his wooden head.

Keeping Pinocchio in school gives Patri a chance to play with the very idea of schooling. Pinocchio, lonely at night, complains,

> "What mistakes I made! I swam the ocean to escape school, and
> here I am in school. I ran away to find freedom and I am a prisoner.

> Poor miserable me. I can never do examples. Why should a man buy
> six hats? One is more than enough. . . . And the spelling? Never shall
> I learn that. It is without sound or sense. Take this morning's lesson.
> He said 'Write "you see me."' I cramp my fingers, and write with
> much pain 'U C Me' . . . (and he says) . . . "Wrong, wrong, how can
> you be so stupid? Write it this way' and to please him a poor mari-
> onette must twist his tongue and cramp his fingers again and again
> in the making of three crooked marks where but one was needed.
> Why write, 'You see me' when you can write 'U C Me'? (p. 95)

Pinocchio's resistance and defiance is in the service of his imagined
freedom. He believes that he should have no restraints or restrictions, and
nothing those who care about him can do will persuade him to become
thoughtful and hard working. The book sets up a tension between those
who care for Pinocchio and the puppet himself. This is quite different
from the tension in Collodi's book, where there are wicked forces constantly tempting him into mischief. Pinocchio in Patri's book is not
tempted into self-indulgence so much as warned that fame and fortune are
not to be found easily in the New World despite the myths of America he
may have heard in Italy.

The book was published in 1928 and Patri, an educator of many Italian
immigrant children and an immigrant himself, must have had them in
mind when he wrote the book. All of Pinocchio's advisors constantly try to
tell him that intelligence and critical thought, looking behind things for
their meaning, and not braggadocio and thoughtless enthusiasm, are
required to make it in a democracy.

Pinocchio persists in his resistance to learning while the Rooster and
the Blue Fairy continue to push him to look behind things for their meanings, learn from his experience, and be considerate to people rather than
expect the world to center around his wants. As Patri put it, "He was living, not thinking." (p. 154)

During the course of the story Pinocchio grows into a more thoughtful,
analytic, compassionate person. He is adopted by godparents and
acquires a loving pet dog. With the guidance of the rooster, the Blue Fairy,
his dog, and caring godparents, Pinocchio becomes a nicer person,
though he retains a mischievous and rebellious streak. He becomes part of
a world larger than himself and begins to welcome his place in it.

Patri's Pinocchio is not rewarded for this by becoming a human boy.

Instead he remains complex, torn between mischief and goodness, some-times thoughtful and sometimes inconsiderate, but basically decent.

Toward the very end of the book a dramatic change comes over Pinoc-chio. He becomes polite and contemplative, a sign in boys, Patri says, that requires a visit from the Doctor, who acknowledges, "When a boy's too polite—m-m-n very bad sign that." (p. 233) Pinocchio is homesick for Italy and tells the doctor he wants to go home to Gepetto. He explains, "I didn't run away from Gepetto. I ran away from school. I thought America was a land where you did what you liked and if you didn't like it you didn't do it. But it is worse than home for going to school."

Homesickness overcomes Pinocchio as it must almost every immigrant to the United States. But Pinocchio is able to return to Gepetto—return in style. The improbable ending of the book has him returning to Italy with the King of Italy. As his ship leaves New York Harbor he sees the Rooster, a scarecrow who helped him, his godmother and godfather: All the people he met on his journey in the United States pull off masks and he sees them as they are, behind the masks—guardian angels, protectors, and teachers. The Statue of Liberty herself leans down to him as he asks her a final ques-tion, "Please tell me what is behind things?" and she answers, "Ques-tions . . . if you want to be happy, you keep on asking questions of whatever, whomever you meet without ever taking the answers as the last word."

And the book ends with Pinocchio's response to Liberty, " 'And what,' thought Pinocchio, 'do you suppose is behind that?' "

There is something admirable about the message of this otherwise ordinary book. Throughout the book Pinocchio is urged to search for meaning, ask questions, learn through doing, and analyze his own experi-ence, all central tenets of progressive education. *Pinocchio in America* is a progressive education parable, a story of learning despite school. It is the only children's fiction I have found written by a person explicitly involved in the progressive education movment of the 1920s and 1930s and, as such, is worth knowing about.

Pinocchio's search for freedom in America was school-obsessed. Yet to the very end he decides that school is not for him, though questioning and looking behind things definitely are. School plays a central role in the lives of immigrants to the United States, both for themselves and for their chil-dren. For some it can be a source of passage into economic success and fuller participation in the mainstream. For others it can be a source of humiliation, failure, and continued marginalization. Patri was very aware of this himself, since writing children's books was just a sideline for him. He was an important, now-neglected educator whose work with poor immigrant children in the first half of the century has much to teach us now.

TAKE 3: ANGELO PATRI, EDUCATOR: AMERICANIZING AMERICA

My first encounter with Angelo Patri, the author of *Pinocchio in America*, was in 1986. I was working with my wife, Judy, on *The Long Haul*, the autobiography of Myles Horton, founder of the Highlander Center. Myles had a way of educating you when you weren't looking, so whenever he asked me to accompany him on a trip I knew that he had both his agenda and one for me. On one occasion he asked me to accompany him to Hidden Villa near Palo Alto, California, to meet Josephine Duvenick, who was ninety-nine at the time. She told me about her seventy-five years of active involvement in progressive education. At the end of the evening we spent together she said she had a few books she thought I would like. One was *A Schoolmaster of the Great City* (New York: Macmillan, 1923) by Angelo Patri. The title seemed archaic, and it took me several years to pick up the book and read it.

Understanding the power that book continues to have for me requires a digression. In 1962 I taught at PS 103 on 118th Street and Madison Avenue in Manhattan. The building was erected in 1895 and still functioned as a school. Only recently I learned that my mother attended that school sometime between 1912 and 1925, when she was growing up in a mostly Italian neighborhood in East Harlem. I wrote about teaching at PS 103 in *36 Children*. That old building, now torn down, represented for me all that was worst in education and most important in my learning how to teach. It was decrepit, the staff was demoralized, the students desperate because their social, cultural, and intellectual lives were impoverished by the education thrown at them.

PS 103 was also the school described by Angelo Patri in *A Schoolmaster of the Great City*. Patri, as far as I can figure out, was principal of 103 at the same time my mother attended the school. The major difference in our times is that the defiant and miseducated children Patri encountered were Italian, Irish, and Jewish, while those I encountered in the same school were African American and Puerto Rican.

The best way I can describe the state of PS 103 when I taught there comes directly from Patri's description of the first school he taught at somewhere else in East Harlem:

> . . . the children were afraid of the teachers, and the teachers feared the children.
>
> The neighborhood was a place from which the teachers escaped, and into which the children burrowed. One never knew as he went through the streets what missile or epithet might greet him. . . .
>
> I do not remember a period in my life when I was more silent and sober minded than during the first six months of my career in this school. Day in and day out I sat quietly scarcely saying an unnecessary word and by gestures rather than speech indicating to the children what I wanted done.
>
> I went through the building silent, rarely speaking. I looked out upon the streets, silent. I visited the shops and listened to the talk of the fathers. I visited some of the homes. Here too, I talked little, trying to get people to talk to me.
>
> The school was failing. I was failing and my whole mind was concentrated upon finding the cause and the remedy.
>
> After school hours I would stare out of the windows and look out upon the strange mixture of people with their prejudices, their sensitiveness and their shiftlessness and ponder upon the gulf between them and me.
>
> There was no attempt on the part of the school to understand the problem and to direct the lives of the pupils. In fact, teaching the curriculum was the routine business of the day—no more. There was apparently little affection for the children, and no interest in the parents as co-workers in their education.

Patri worked with Pinocchio and his friends. At the time he taught in East Harlem the concentration of people per square mile was greater than that in Naples or Rome. There were over 100,000 Italian immigrant families in the community. In addition, there were tens of thousands of immigrant Jews and Irish. Almost all the Jewish and Italian children went to public school, though many of the Irish children attended Catholic schools. Patri was himself an immigrant from Italy and didn't enter school in New

York until he was eleven years old. Not surprisingly, Patri begins *Schoolmaster* with a story about stories he heard while he was a child in Italy:

> I remember sitting with the family and the neighbors' families about the fireplace, while father, night after night, told us stories of the Knights of the Crusades or recounted the glories of the heroes of proud Italy.
>
> How he could tell a story! His voice was strong and soft, and soothing, and he had just sufficient power of exaggeration to increase the attractiveness of the tale. We could see the soldiers he told us about pass before us in all their struggles and sorrows and triumphs. Back and forth he marched them into Asia Minor, across Sicily, and into the castles of France, Germany and England. We listened eagerly and came back each night ready to be thrilled and inspired again by the spirit of the good and the great.
>
> Then came the journey over the sea, and the family with the neighbors' families were part of the life of New York. We were Little Italy.

It is easy to forget that Italian immigrants in New York at the turn of the century faced the same problems of crowding and poverty, and the same linguistic bewilderment, that current immigrants face. Many of these immigrant families came from places where there was greater social coherence than any found in the United States, and people from the same communities or regions tended to cluster together and re-create the social ties of small villages whenever possible. I experienced a bit of this in the Bronx growing up in the 1940s. Until I was about six, our life resembled that of a rural Jewish East European village. My grandparents, whom my mother and father shared a house with, were surrounded by landsmen—people who had come from the same part of Europe as they did and who spoke Yiddish with the same accent and had the same politics as they did. I noticed a similar situation for many of the Puerto Rican families I taught in New York during the sixties. People lived in extended families and communities that had cultural and geographic ties on the island.

Life in the United States disrupted and often destroyed social cohesion as people moved away for work or for better living conditions, or married out. Too many so-called experts identify poverty with lack of social cohesion when often the opposite is true, the acquisition of wealth leading to the breakdown of communities. This is not to advocate or romanticize poverty so much as to point out that social mobility often leads to social instability. Patri remarks:

The colony life of the city's immigrants is an attempt to continue the village traditions of the mother country. In our neighborhood there were hundreds of families that had come from the same part of Italy. On summer nights they gathered in groups on the sidewalks, the stoops, the court-yards, and talked and sang and dreamed. In winter the men and boys built Roman arches out of the snow.

But gradually the families grew in size. The neighborhood became congested. A few families moved away. Ours was one of them. We began to be a part of the new mass instead of the old. The city with its tremendous machinery, its many demands, its constant calling, calling, began to take hold. What had been intimate, quaint, beautiful, ceased to appeal.

One institution that has often contributed to the breakdown of the social fabric of poor immigrant (and Native American) communities is school. The idea of becoming schooled as an American, abandoning other cultural roots and identity, created distances between immigrants and their children. However, it often did not contribute to the integration of these immigrants and their children into the majority community. Jews, for example, may have become economically successful, but in Christian America we remain Jews nevertheless. This is also the case, though perhaps to a lesser degree, with Italians, Greeks, Lebanese, and many Eastern Europeans. It is even more dramatically true for people of color, for Latinos, African Americans, and Asian Americans. School has traditionally not taught the children of immigrants their parents' languages or cultures. Nor, until recently, has cultural respect been placed at the center of the curriculum.

The tension between maintaining one's cultural distinctness and becoming a part of the American mix has existed from the beginning of public education in the United States. As a consequence, there have been struggles for cultural diversity on local and regional levels throughout the past. For example, in the mid-nineteenth century many German immigrant communities in the Midwest successfully fought for the teaching of German language and culture in public schools. And in the 1930s and 1940s Patri and his friend and colleague Leonard Covello led a successful fight for the development of Italian studies, clubs, and classes, and the teaching of the Italian language in the New York City public schools. It was the first major battle for cultural diversity fought in the New York City public schools.

Patri knew about the problems of language, culture, and social coherence in immigrant communities firsthand. His first language was Italian, and he didn't attend public school until he was eleven. As he recounts in his book:

> I was eleven before I went to a city school. All the English I knew had been learned in the street. I knew Italian. From the time I was seven I had written letters for the neighbors. Especially the women-folk took me off to a corner and asked me to write letters to their friends in Italy. As they told me the story I wrote it down. I thus learned the beat of plain folks' hearts.
>
> My uncle from whom I had learned Italian went back to Italy and I was left without a teacher, so one day I attached myself to a playmate and went to school; an "American" school. I gave my name and my age and was told to sit in a long row of benches with some sixty other children. The teacher stood at the blackboard and wrote "March 5, 1887."

Patri did not intend to teach but became a teacher by default. He tells the story of his fall into teaching:

> I went to school, father went to work, mother looked after the house. When evening came, instead of sitting about the fire, talking and reliving the day, we sat, each in his own corner. One nursed his tired bones, another prepared his lessons for the morrow. The demands of the school devoured me; the work world exhausted my father. The long evenings of close contact with my home people were becoming rare. I was slipping away from my home; home was slipping away from me.
>
> Yet my father knew what he was about. While the fathers of most of the boys about me were putting their money into business or into their houses, mine put his strength, his love, his money, his comforts into making me better than himself. The spirit of the crusaders should live again in his son. He wanted me to become a priest: I wanted to become a doctor.
>
> During all the years that he worked for me, I worked for myself. While his hopes were centered in the family, mine were extending beyond it. I worked late into the nights, living a life of which my father was not a part. This living by myself tended to make me forget, indeed to undervalue, the worth of my people. I was ashamed sometimes because my folk did not look or talk like Americans.
>
> When most depressed by the feeling of living crudely and poorly, I would go out to see my father at work. I would see him

high up on a scaffold a hundred feet in the air and my head would
get dizzy and my heart would rise to my throat. Then I would think
of him once more as the poet storyteller with the strong, soothing
voice and the far-off vision eye, and the poet in his soul would link
itself to mine, and would see why on two-dollar-a-day wages he
sent me to college.

Proud of his strength I would strengthen my moral fiber and
respond to his dream. Yet not as he dreamed, for when he fell fifty
feet down a ladder and was ill for a whole year I went to work at
teaching.

A Schoolmaster of the Great City goes on to describe how Patri came to
love teaching, not as he found it in the schools but as he and other progressives re-created it. He attended Teachers College, Columbia, during John
Dewey's tenure there and was part of a group of young progressives who
worked to transform ghetto schools in New York into progressive, community-based, respectful, and respected places of learning. Patri's students, most of whom were considered troublemakers, incapable of
learning, and all of whom were of Irish, Italian, Puerto Rican, and Jewish
backgrounds, thrived in what was called in those days a "New School."
Patri achieved on a schoolwide scale what I attempted in my single classroom forty years later in the same building at a time when the students
were all African American and Puerto Rican. At the center of his transfor-
mative work were stories—his stories, his students' stories, and the stories
of the community he served. He describes how he discovered this power
of stories to transform learning:

When the principal assigned the assembly exercises and the discipline of the school to me, I was glad. I had learned to believe in
children. I had begun to analyze my own childhood more carefully.
Here was an opportunity to test my knowledge in a larger way than
the classroom offered.

I began by telling the boys what a fine assembly was like in other
schools. Once more I resorted to stories. They never failed. Father
had done his share nobly. The big restless crowd settled down and
listened. As each day went by, cautiously I put the problem of
school discipline before them and they responded by taking over
much of the responsibility for it themselves. A sort of council was
held in my room each week at which the problems of the school
were discussed. From fifty to one hundred of the most responsible
boys in the school attended, and as there were only about twelve

hundred in all, the representatives were fairly adequate to the need.

This experience helped me wonderfully. Through it I gained increased confidence in the children, in the power of the school, in myself. (p. 22)

Every child has a story to tell, and within that story is the secret of reaching her or him as a learner. Sometimes that inner story is revealed through writing or painting or through some action a child takes or a decision he or she makes that reveals character. Sometimes children don't value their stories, or don't know them until they are given an opportunity to tell them. Sometimes their stories are neglected or insulted. And sometimes, as too often happens in school, they are silenced. Yet there are schools where stories are encouraged, where speaking is honored in all its complex manifestations, and where all the creative efforts of students are respected. These are places where, for children, there are adults there for them, adults who listen, look, and learn as well as teach.

Patri seemed to have an uncanny ear for children's stories, primarily, I believe, because he was looking for them. As a teacher and principal, he searched to understand the dreams and aspirations of his students, and set up circumstances for them to share their own experiences. I imagine him telling the tales of Pinocchio to his students and encouraging them to make up new adventures for Pinocchio. In *Schoolmaster* he mentions "magic carpets" in some of the primary school rooms, places where storytelling was honored. It seems that one of his joys as a principal, and evidently his students' joys too, was for him to stop into different classes and tell stories.

Stories transport students to worlds beyond their own-often troubled one. They encourage them to become intimate with their own imaginations and explore what they might like to be as well as understand who they are. And for the listener who is also an educator, children's stories are windows into their uniqueness and clues on how to connect the child and the curriculum. Sometimes children's own stories are difficult to uncover, and in rare cases they are lost or dead. Often they demand that the school change, that rules be broken or new opportunities provided. Caring educators value their students' stories more than they value the rules and rituals they create to keep a classroom or school orderly. It is through stories and the action they lead to that discipline problems can disappear and the so-called problem of discipline be turned into the challenge of remaking the school for the students. What this means is going beyond the curriculum, taking time to listen, and knowing people.

Not only children have stories: Parents and communities have stories, and teachers, too, have tales to tell. In a learning community where everyone cares about everyone else's story, respect and affection can flourish. It is amazing to me how even the most unsocialized people will recognize a situation where people treat each other decently, care about what each has to say, and know something of everybody's story.

Patri is very clear on mischief in the classroom and its relationship to the neglect of needs and the frustration of dreams. He describes the dissipation of discipline problems at his school in the following way:

> What had become of the problem of school discipline, the friction that resulted when a teacher tried to teach and a child would not learn? I had begun by punishing children that were reported, by all the means known to schoolmasters; detention, reprimand, lowered standing, suspension from work, parents' assistance, but following the child into the street and home had changed the point of view. The problem of making the child behave had become the problem of providing the best conditions of growth for him. The school discipline had given way to life discipline—and appreciation of social values, because the children that needed discipline needed the help of the community, the people, the teachers, the doctors.

Patri illustrates this with the story of Jacob, a boy of nine or ten who constantly ran away from school. Nothing Patri did kept Jacob from running away until something surprising happened. According to Patri:

> Jacob discovered a teacher he liked. She was teaching the first grade and a girls' class. Jacob was in the second grade, thanks to the truant school, but when he discovered Miss Katherine, instead of making his way out of the building he appeared disheveled and dusty beside her.
>
> "I want to be in your class."
>
> "But," said the astonished Miss Katherine, "this is a girls' class and a first grade."
>
> "Where will I sit?" asked Jacob.
>
> Before the teacher could recover herself, Jacob had found an empty seat and taken it as if to say, "Let the world roll on, I'm happy."
>
> The big man had lost his job. No matter how often Jacob was

placed in his right class he found his way to Miss Katherine's room. There was only one thing to do and that was to let him stay with her. Miss Katherine understood Jacob. He loved growth and the smell of growing things. He wanted to handle flowers, dirt, animals, and Miss Katherine saw that he got the chance. She understood what happened to Jacob on fine spring mornings when the roll was called and Jacob did not answer. She sent him on trips to his beloved woods and he brought back treasures of the outdoors. These he tended.

When he at last recognized that he had outgrown Miss Katherine's class he took his proper grade but reported daily to his first friend.

We were thankful Miss Katherine belonged to our school. While she took care of Jacob, the rest of us had grasped a new idea. We made a point of assigning the troublesome child to a teacher whom he liked. The teacher friend kept in touch with him as long as she could be useful. Sometimes the child outgrew one advisor and was assigned to another. Oftener the relationship lasted through his school life and beyond it.

Jacob revealed his story and Patri and Miss Katherine listened. And she learned of his love of growth and need for security and nurtured it. Patri not merely allowed Jacob to break the rules but went beyond that and watched and listened to what happened to Jacob to draw a larger conclusion, one that applied to other youngsters and to the structure and functioning of the school itself. He initiated genuine grass-roots change at the school. He learned from Jacob, analyzed what happened, and then generalized in a way that led to the greater personalization and democratization of the school.

The personalization of education has to be distinguished from the individualization of learning, which is an invidious form of cultural and social isolation. Through the individualization of learning each student is considered an isolate who has a unique learning program shaped for her or him. In addition, the individualized learning program is a form of channeling, of shaping what each individual learns without respecting any input from the learner or criticism from the group. It is preparation for work at a computer workstation or at a fast-food restaurant. The child is not part of a caring community of learners, nor is she or he involved in a collective quest for knowledge. Communication in a group is neglected as are the essential skills of storytelling, listening, and understanding.

A community of learners is premised on the full appreciation of each person within the group. It requires attention to each person's voice and stories, common learning experiences, as well as an appreciation of the private person and individual learning preferences. Very few educational leaders have the courage or sense to listen and learn and rebuild their schools based on what the needs of their students and community are—as communities of learning.

Patri did that. He listened as much to the stories of his students' parents as he did to the students themselves and began to conceive of the school as a center of community life. In a way, he tried to build a school for Gepetto, the Blue Fairy, Pinocchio, and all the families he served, no matter how difficult the circumstances of their lives or their culture. In *Schoolmaster* it becomes clear that Patri honored the culture and person of all the families he served.

A school as the center of community life was imagined not only by Patri but also by his friend Leonard Covello, who did on a high school level what Patri did in elementary school. Covello's school, Benjamin Franklin High School, was built for him by the New York City Board of Education and was a short walk from Patri's school. The work of these two Italian progressive educators is not well enough known, and it is worth pausing here, in the midst of the story of Pinocchio and Patri's school, to tell a bit of Covello's story as well.

Leonard Covello was himself an Italian immigrant. He was born in 1887 in the small, impoverished Italian town of Avigliano not far from Naples. In his autobiography, *The Heart Is the Teacher* (with Guido D'Agostino, [New York: McGraw-Hill, 1958]), he describes his early childhood:

> I was born and grew up among the men who had fought in the wars of Italian renunciation. My uncles, cousins, and other relatives related stories about Mazzini and Garibaldi and particularly about the brigands who inhabited the region of Lucania—stories told around the fireplace with just the light from the burning logs. Children listened to their elders. We rarely ventured even a question and never offered a comment, for that was the way to absorb knowledge and wisdom. Duty was stressed. *"E il tuo dovere!"* "It is your duty!" It was your duty to prepare for a useful life.

At the age of nine, in 1896, Covello, his mother, and his younger brothers were able to emigrate to New York when Covello's father, who was already in America, sent money for passage. Leonard grew up in East Harlem, to return there in 1933 when pressure brought by his friend, recently elected Mayor Fiorello La Guardia, and his former student, U.S. Representative Vito Marcantonio, persuaded the New York City Board of Education to build a community high school in East Harlem and appoint Covello principal.

Before that, from the early 1910s, Covello had taught English, French, and then Italian at De Witt Clinton High School, which was then located at 59th Street and 10th Avenue on the West Side of Manhattan. Covello's Italian classes at Clinton were the first to be taught in the New York City public schools. When Covello started teaching, Italian was considered a language not fit to be taught in the high schools. Greek, Latin, French, and sometimes Spanish were the academic languages, and Italian was looked upon as a street language, one with no cultural importance. Covello led the fight to create Italian clubs (they were called Circolos) at Clinton and to get the board of education to approve the teaching of Italian. His battle was one of the first explicit struggles in the United States over multiculturalism and ethnic studies in the high schools.

In order to achieve his goal, Covello visited the parents of his high school students, and in his autobiography he described one of these visits this way:

> Our visits usually turned into lessons in democracy, trying to make the immigrant understand his rights and privileges. "Would you prefer your son to study Italian, or some other foreign language?" "What a question! Naturally, we prefer him to study our own language. But *real* Italian. Italian as you speak it, Signor Maestro—the Italian of our great men, of Garibaldi.

In May 1922 Covelo's battle to legitimize teaching Italian was finally won. As he says in his autobiography:

> I had longed for the day when I would have just one class in Italian to teach. Never did I imagine that in the space of a few years there would be hundreds of boys studying Italian at Clinton—and that there would be five teachers in the Italian Department.

Covello's relationship with his students was key to his future work at Ben Franklin. He was storyteller, listener, teacher, grandfather, neighbor, community activist, and scholar. One of the members of his Circolo at Clinton and eventually his lifelong friend, Congressman Vito Marcantonio, gave Covello the nickname "Pop," one that lasted throughout his career.

I mention this story because of incidents that occurred when I was involved with the parent school board in East Harlem during the 1960s struggles for community control of schools. A number of the board members, African American and Puerto Rican, not Italian, used to tell me that they were going to visit Pop and ask for his advice whenever the struggle seemed particularly difficult and the best strategy unclear. After a while I asked them who this Pop was, and it turned out to be Covello, their old high school principal. As one of them told me, they knew their struggles were his struggles, and they trusted him to share his advice and wisdom with them.

From 1931 to 1933 plans developed for a high school in East Harlem. Many school people argued for a vocational school, claiming that it was the best thing for a poor and largely immigrant community. Covello disagreed and succeeded in allowing an experimental high school to be created in the community, the same community, by the way, that Central Park East High School currently serves. This high school would cross lines between academic and vocational education and would, in Covello's words, "have all the dignity of a seat of learning, . . . reflect its influence into the community and be the center for its improvement." (p. 181)

The central goal of Benjamin Franklin High School was to become an integral part of its community and to provide ways and means by which the school and community might work together for the good of the children and of the community at large. According to Covello, the school was

> dedicated to the service of youth in an immigrant area; to the development, in the American manner, of a community that sprang into being through the isolation of the foreign-born from the American way of living; to the preservation of basic values in the cultural heritages of the racial groups that form the Population of the East Harlem community; to the eradication of the sense of inferiority . . . that sets up barriers both to the happiness of isolated groups and to their realization of our national ideals. It is dedicated to the creation of a common understanding of, and a common loyalty to, the American ideal, and to a restoration of communal living in which neighborliness and mutual helpfulness shall contribute to progress, happiness, and wholesome living in East

Harlem, the small city . . . encompassed by the vastness of the greater city of New York. . . . This district has an identity of its own, in addition to which its area is definitely prescribed with boundaries that are recognized by all. Such boundaries make it easier to consider it, not as a segregated community in a large city, but as a town within the great city in which community life may be reestablished by applying an American program, conceived in the American spirit with all the friendliness possible.

With this statement Covello articulated the marriage of cultural diversity with an American sensibility, which Patri also talked about. Covello's placement of cultural integrity directly alongside a sense of belonging to a diverse democratic whole is one of the earliest statements advocating multicultural learning that I know of, and his practice of the idea was pioneering. In *The Heart Is the Teacher* he describes some of the things done at Franklin:

At Ben Franklin we conducted assembly programs in which lectures were given by prominent people from each culture group, as well as entertainment and exhibitions of art and music. Dr. Scott Mijakawa spoke on Japan's contribution to civilization. I introduced the Puerto Rican assemblies where there were music and dancing by Puerto Rican artists, singing and dancing by Puerto Rican high-school girls, and education talks by Dr. Abraham Kroll, who had taught for several years in Puerto Rico.

Dr. Rachel Davis-Dubois instructed the teachers in classroom work on intercultural relations. I remember her saying, "Much can be done in the classroom to foster changes in attitudes while enriching the day-by-day routine."

Facts omitted in ordinary textbooks and reading materials were woven into the regular work.

We tackled the problem of improving intercultural relations at Franklin in many ways. Often after assembly, a few selected students came to my office and had the opportunity over a cup of tea, of talking to a Japanese actor, or a Jewish rabbi, or a Negro poet. One Irish lad, after shaking hands and saying a few words to Dr. Mijakawa, whispered to me, "Gee, Pop, he's just like anybody else!"

Just how valuable all this activity was could be argued interminably. It has been said that it sometimes takes fifty years for an educational idea to take hold and become accepted as an integral part of school work.

This last statement of Covello's was prophetic.

If a school is to be a center of community learning it must know the community it serves and collaborate with members of the community to develop educational programs. It is not adequate to pick and choose among the best of commercially produced materials and programs available. Rather, on a school-by-school basis, practice should be tailor-made to meet the needs of the students and the community. Covello says that, in order to realize this,

> As a first move, the school undertook to secure adequate information about the East Harlem community in which it is located. . . . Surveys by those sympathetic to the community and to the work to be done were tactfully and informally made. Home visits and personal interviews with parents became a part of the regular school program. All available data on the East Harlem neighborhood were studied thoroughly. Statistical information of all kinds was assembled, and a series of maps showing racial distribution in the community was prepared. Likewise, social maps were drawn showing the location of every school, church, social and civic agency. These provided a background of information for those who were undertaking the task of transforming all such necessary details into a program humanly helpful in which the emphasis is placed not on records, statistics, and routine plans but upon human values both in the school and in the community.

This information was understood as telling part of the story of the community. The survey was not a cold statistical study but a composite and complex portrait of a living community, one that deserved an education fitted to its complexities and its needs. Communities have multiple stories, and it is unfortunate that so much of education neglects community-specific matters that influence how students learn and what they want and need to know. A caring education must be one in which the nature of life, both individual and communal, is taken into account. This doesn't always mean reinforcing everything in a community, since there are negative as well as positive aspects of communal living. Rather it means that, consistent with principles of equity and justice, life within the community will be respected and honored, and that communal needs will help shape the curriculum and the structure of schooling.

Educators and schools also have stories, and Patri and Covello in their books tell the stories of two schools in the same community at about the same time (Patri's was about a decade earlier). Both of these stories portray a number of journeys: the journey from Italy to the United States; the journey of an immigrant boy though the schools in America to become a teacher; and the journey to remake education so it serves the school's community of students and parents; and finally the journey to remake America as a more just place within which cultural differences are respected. As Patri says of the role of schools: "Americanize the foreigner, nay; through the child let us fulfill our destiny and Americanize America." (p. 219)

Covello describes his educational voyage in a way that applies equally to Patri:

> I have tried to show how, though at first I was only concerned with books and the imparting of information, ultimately I came to realize how the heart and mind not only of the individual boy but of his whole community are involved in the education process.

Implicit in all these tales is the idea that the education of a person is an unfolding and lifelong story. Collodi's *Pinocchio* is the tale of a puppet's voyage to personhood. Patri's *Pinocchio in America* is an elaboration on that tale centered on the role of education in the development of humane sensibility. They are both stories about the education of a boy who hates school and yet is smart, curious, full of mischief, and good of heart. They illustrate the way school, community, and family together shape personality and set the context for growth and development. Patri's and Covello's autobiographical books are immigrant stories with a difference. They are not tales about successful integration into American society but tales about the need immigrants perceive to make the society they come to more democratic through education. In both of them it is the immigrant who is the source of democratic transformation, and it is the cultural sensibilities brought by the immigrant in search of the dream of tolerance and democracy that is healing for America.

These two Italian progressive educators have an important message for those of us who are struggling these days to develop multicultural education and an appreciation of the values of diversity in the context of school. They make it clear that it is incumbent upon educators who embark on change to take the communities they serve along with them as full participants. They also remind us that students—people—are not disposable.

Community is the center of coherent life. Culture is, for many peoples, the source of their strength to survive poverty and oppression. And the public schools have been and continue to be, however unreasonable it sometimes seems, sources of hope. When we embark upon changing them we must look at the best practices of the past and the most visionary of current dreams. And we must consider and critique them ruthlessly and with loving care. The role of education in the making of democracy is crucial, and we cannot lightly give up the responsibility for other people's children and for their dreams—a responsibility we have accepted by choosing to teach in the public schools. Nor can we afford to forget the Patris and Covellos, who made in the past and in different circumstances, the same struggles that need to be made today. We must honor the sense of mischief and adventure that Pinocchio brings to the table, because struggles for social justice are not without components of righteous mischief and moral adventure.

In the last chapter of *A Schoolmaster of the Great City*, Angelo Patri gives some advice on how to create new schools to deal with old problems, schools that are multicultural and humana, that listen to the stories of children, and communities, and teachers, and are the result of creative collaborations of caring people. We would do well to heed this advice:

> The school must constantly ask, "What is the effect of my programme on the soul growth of the children? Why is it that my programme does not reach all children? What can I do to keep in touch with ideas that are vigorous and young? What can I do to keep sane, human, far-seeing? How can I respect the child's prolonged infancy and keep him from facing the struggle of the labour market until he is mentally and physically fit? How can I translate efficiency, goodness, will training, citizenship, parental duty into child happiness?
>
> The child is the permanent factor.

THE GOOD OLD DAYS.
I WAS THERE. WHERE WAS THEY?
A FICTIONAL HISTORY OF PUBLIC
EDUCATION IN THE UNITED STATES

Free public education that provides opportunity for all children in our country is part of the story of American democracy. My grandparents came to this country not so much because of what it could offer them as for what it could offer their children. Neither of them ever took advantage of the opportunity for education, but their children and grandchildren did, and it made a considerable difference in our families' lives. To this day my father contributes to his college out of gratitude for the free education it provided for him when his family was very poor. He swears by what the schools used to be, and yet admits at times that all the schools of his day weren't that good and that there were schools he attended that were no different from the public schools now. However, he and many, many people believe in the good old days of public education when all students learned, when there were no discipline problems, and when all the schools were run in one effective way and provided the skills needed for adult life in the United States. Whenever I hear the phrase "the good old days," however, I think of something the comedienne Moms Mabley used to say: "The good old days. I was there. Where was they?"

People want to believe in the good old days. It is an assertion of the belief that there was a time when all the institutions of American democracy functioned smoothly, and that current problems are just temporary aberrations. Regarding the schools, it is a reassertion of the idea that every child should have the opportunity to be successful in life. When we cease to believe in democracy, we lose faith in ourselves as a nation. Our strength is not ultimately the strength of our weapons or propaganda. It will come only from our ability to realize the democratic dreams of the people who struggled in the eighteenth century to make us a nation.

At times of loss of faith—and we are now experiencing a loss of faith in public institutions like the schools—it is comfortable to turn to the past to reaffirm so-called traditional values. Yet the very notion of a homogeneous past is a construction that has little regard for actual history. The history of the United States has been, among other things, the story of a struggle to achieve democracy, not the story of democracy triumphant. This is as true of public education as it is of the economy, politics, and culture. As Benjamin Rush, one of the signers of the Declaration of Independence and a founder of the first antislavery society in the United States, said in 1787:

> There is nothing more common than to confound the terms of *American Revolution* with those of the late *American War.* The American war is over, but this is far from being the case with the American revolution. On the contrary, nothing but the first act of the great drama is closed.

One central theme of Act Two of the American Revolution was the development of free basic education. We did not begin with any models. Free public education was invented in the United States, and it is worth going back to that postrevolutionary moment when education was considered essential to the development of an American democracy. There we shall look at the origins of progressive education within the context of the creation of public schools. Contrary to popular knowledge, progressive education is not a product of the late nineteenth century, or of the thirties or sixties, any more than progressive politics is a recent invention. People in our society have never agreed upon what is basic for education in a democracy. It is definitely worth taking a look at where we have been in order to illuminate where we are and what we need to do in the next twenty-five years to revitalize public education and reaffirm our faith in democracy.

Over the last seven years I've been researching the history of education in the United States to learn the origins of the progressive traditions in which I work. This adventure into our educational past has been exciting, and the only way to condense it is through telling a story. I created an American teaching family (there are actually many teaching families) that struggled to build public education from the beginning of our existence as a nation. I have tried to capture the spirit of the struggle to create public education, and through that, to ensure democracy in our nation. I hope it will help those people currently engaged in the struggle to know and honor the tradition of which they are a part. The story begins in

Turin, Ohio, a fictional town somewhere in eastern Ohio near the Pennsylvania border:

EDUCATION IN TURIN: A FICTIONAL NARRATIVE

All of the old Pennsylvania people claimed an acquaintance with Benjamin Franklin, but Elizabeth believed that her grandfather, Jonathan Stokes, was the only one whose stories were convincing enough to make it plausible. Elizabeth was a teacher and loved to hear her grandfather tell teaching tales.

Jonathan Stokes was born in Philadelphia in 1760. In 1776, at the age of sixteen, he joined the Pennsylvania militia on their mad march to Amboy, New Jersey, to support Washington's effort to hold New York. He was wounded in the right leg and, as his friends used to joke, limped his way through the whole Revolutionary War.

Stokes was one of Philadelphia's seasonal soldiers. During the winters from 1777 to 1783 he apprenticed as a printer. During the springs and summers he fought with the Pennsylvania militia, which by the end of the war was as good a fighting unit as any in the world.

After the war, Jonathan Stokes worked as a printer in Philadelphia, trying to scrape enough money together to buy his own press and type and set himself up as a printer. It was during that time, he told anyone who would listen, that he met Franklin. He had been invited by another printer to join the Leather Apron for an evening of discussion at a local tavern.

The Leather Apron was the name adopted by members of the self-education group set up by Benjamin Franklin to distinguish themselves from the Merchant's Every Night, which was composed of older and richer citizens, and the Bachelor's, which was a drinking club. Franklin's group, whose formal name was the Junto, consisted of working people—joiners, printers, surveyors, shoemakers—who were serious about science, politics, education, community service, and, in its early years, revolution.

The Junto met once a week in a local tavern. Questions were set for study and research for the next meeting, and then the previous week's questions were discussed, with occasional pauses for toasts and rounds of ale. Jonathan Stokes said that what delighted him most about Franklin's circle was the combination of humor and seriousness. They discussed questions such as "Whence comes the Dew that stands on the outside of a Tankard that has cold Water in it in the Summer Time"; "If a Sovereign Power attempts to deprive a Subject of his Right (or which is the same thing, of what he thinks is his Right) is it justifiable in him to resist if he is able?"; "Does it not in a general Way require a great Study and intense Application for a Poor Man to become rich and Powerful, if he would do it, without the Forfeiture of his Honesty?"[1] In the midst of these discussions they joked, drank, and brought up proposals for their mutual assistance and for ways of aiding the Philadelphia community. It was through these discussions that the idea of a public lending library grew, and through their reverence for the printed word that Jonathan learned the importance of building up and sharing a collection of books.

One of Jonathan's prized possessions was a copy of Benjamin Franklin's *Proposals Relating to the Education of Youth in Pennsylvania*. It was hard to get a copy, as it was printed in 1749, but Jonathan was able to trade with an older printer several evenings' work for a copy. The education of the young was one of Jonathan's obsessions though he had no formal schooling himself. In a way, he was relieved he didn't have to attend the schools he observed, as they treated students harshly and didn't encourage the boldness and inventiveness Jonathan believed the new nation needed. He found a footnote in Franklin's book that struck something deep within him and he memorized it. The footnote was a quote from a Mr. Hutcheson, who was a professor in Glasgow during the 1690s:

> The principal end of education is, to form us wise and good creatures, useful to others, and happy ourselves. The whole art of education lies within a narrow compass, and is reducible to a very simple practice; namely, to assist in unfolding those natural and moral powers with which man is endowed, by presenting proper objects and occasions; to watch their growth that they be not diverted from their end, or disturbed in their operation by any foreign violence; and gently to conduct and apply them to all the purposes of private and public life.

There was a lot of movement west in the 1790s. People like Jonathan Stokes felt constrained on the East Coast. There were too many printers in Philadelphia, too little opportunity. Ohio was opening up, growing, might even become a state. The Stokes family moved to eastern Ohio and settled in the small town of Turin (pronounced *Tour in* by the settlers).

The town had been settled by people from Connecticut, though it had Virginians who had fought in Ohio during the war, some French people, remnants of the Indian communities, a small number of free blacks, and a recent influx of Pennsylvania migrants. People kept to their own kind and their own churches. Jonathan, because he was the only printer in town, knew almost everybody. He printed notices, stationery, advertisements, posters. His shop sold books, soap, candles, and was also the town post office. After a while it seemed natural that he be town clerk when, in 1802, Ohio became a state and things began to get a bit more formal. By virtue of being town clerk, another job — superintendent of schools — became Jonathan's. There was no school bureaucracy in those days and in many communities no public schools. The town clerk assumed all the responsibilities for administering public services, including the schools.

Stokes spent more and more time on school matters. He set up a small group like Franklin's Junto, but he associated with the Society of Freemasons. They worked to develop a school and small lending library in Turin. They encountered many problems, especially with the school. Some church people didn't approve of mixing children together. Others worried about whether the secular teachings of the Freemasons and nondenominational deists would be part of the curriculum. Then there was the problem of what to do with the children of the free slaves, and of the demands of immigrants from western Pennsylvania who wanted their children to be taught in German.

The creation of free public schools for all children raised in Turin, as it did throughout the nation, all the complex problems of how a democracy could be forged out of such a mixture of nations, races, and classes.

Jonathan Stokes was surprised and delighted when his granddaughter Elizabeth, who was just sixteen, volunteered to teach at the first public school in Turin. Elizabeth was almost as old as the new century, born in 1812. She was considered a special child. Her grandfather remarked that she must have come into the world reading, and always reminded her that Benjamin Franklin used to comment that he never remembered a time when he couldn't read.

Elizabeth used to spend hours in her grandfather's library, and by the time she was eleven she discussed all the questions brought up at the

Masons' meetings with him. She took care of her cousins and younger brothers and sisters and felt that teaching, having fun with children, and exploring the would were some of the things she enjoyed doing most. A footnote from the book by Benjamin Franklin that her grandfather always quoted stuck with her and formed the basis of her teaching when she took charge of the one-room school at Turin in 1828:

> I say that even children are capable of studying nature, for they have eyes and don't want curiosity; they ask questions, and love to be informed; and here we need only awaken and keep up in them the desire of learning and knowing, which is natural to all mankind. Besides this study, if it is to be called a study, instead of being painful and tedious, is pleasant and agreeable . . . it is inconceivable how many things children are capable of, if all the opportunities and instructing them were laid hold of, with which they themselves supply us.

Elizabeth began her work in a small shed behind the print shop/post office. Her one regret was that the four Black children in Turin were excluded from the school, but she hoped when she was older that she could do something about that. She was committed to the development of common schools, of free schools for all children. She considered herself liberal and enlightened, and valued having children read and learn to think. Reading was a way to keep up with the developments in the larger world, and to develop the spirit of inquiry. For her as for Franklin and other early Americans, an inquiring mind was a powerful tool in a new country where one's opportunities were limited only by one's intelligence and diligence.

As soon as twenty families supported her work, she requested that they build her a schoolhouse. The one-room school was built with donated labor and furniture, and was supported by income from the sale of the land set aside by the federal government in Ohio's statehood charter to support public education. The school was, for many people in the community, a symbol that their dream of a democratic society would be realized, through education, by their children and grandchildren.

The other school in town was more fundamentalist. It grew out of a sectarian, traditionalist church. As John Clayton, the teacher, put it, "The role of education is to instill respect for the Bible, discipline, and the spirit of hard work." John's school started in the home of his brother, a minister, and then moved to the social hall of the newly constructed church. In 1827, when a school tax of one dollar a year on each householder was established, John also asked the parents of the children he served to build a schoolhouse. As was quite common at the time, two one-room schools were built in different parts of the community.

John and Elizabeth had different notions of what common schools should be, and their work reflected those differences, though both were highly respected in the community.

The atmosphere of Elizabeth's school was informal, more like a home than a formal place of learning. She had students who ranged in age from seven to sixteen help each other and take responsibility for keeping the school in good repair. Elizabeth read novels to her students and kept them up on local and national political events. Her family were abolitionists, and every year she taught lessons on the evils of slavery. She told her students that she voted to take in a free Black student one day even though state law prohibited mixed schools.

Elizabeth had been teaching for almost ten years when something happened that changed her life. In 1836, Calvin Stowe, then a professor at the Western Literary Insitute and College of Professional Teachers in Cincinnati, was sent to study schools in Europe by the Ohio state legislature. Stowe was born in 1802, the year of Ohio's admission into the Union. As Stowe said in his report to the legislature,

> In some of the old communities of central Europe, where it happened to be known that I was born in the same year in which Ohio became a sovereign state, it seemed to be a matter of amusement as well as gratification, that a man who was just as old as the state in which he lived, had come with official authority to inquire respecting the best mode of education for the growing population of his native land; and they remarked that our Governor and Legislators must be very enlightened and highly cultivated men.[2]

The Report on Elementary Public Instruction in Europe was submitted to the Thirty-sixth General Assembly of the State of Ohio, December 19, 1837. Ten thousand copies of the report were printed and distributed to every school district in the state. In the report, Stowe urged the establishment of common schools throughout Ohio and said:

> Shall this object (of creating an excellent free system of education),
> then, so desirable in itself, so entirely practicable, so easily within
> our reach, fail of accomplishment? For the honor and welfare of
> our state, for the safety of our whole nation, I trust it will not fail;
> but that soon we shall witness in this commonwealth the introduc-
> tion of a system of common school instruction, fully adequate to
> all the wants of our population.

The Stowe report was received in Turin late in 1837 by Jonathan Stokes, the town clerk and superintendent of schools. He gave it to Elizabeth before reading it himself. She sat down to read it one night and came to the realization, like many teachers in the 1830s and 1840s, that what she had been doing intuitively was part of a tradition to democratize societies through the schools that dated back to Europe in the seventeenth century and perhaps even earlier. She also learned from Stowe that a great deal had been written about educational theory and practice that she had no access to. She determined to learn more about education and improve her prac-tice and decided to spend a summer in Cincinnati at the Western Literary Insitute and College of Professional Teachers, where Stowe and his col-leagues were offering a summer teachers insitute.

Cincinnati changed Elizabeth's life, or at least that's what she always said. At the institute she met Stowe himself and his father-in-law, Lyman Beecher. The whole Beecher family overwhelmed her with their fervor and their eccentricity. In Catherine Beecher, Lymans oldest child, she met the most remarkable woman she'd ever encountered. They took walks together and Catherine con-vinced her of the importance of education for women. Elizabeth's first interest in women's issues came through the Beechers, and though later on she felt Catherine put too much emphasis on the domestic role of the woman, she always read Catherine's books and attended her lectures whenever possible.

Henry Ward, one of the sons, impressed her with the eloquence of his language and the vehemence with which he opposed slavery. Harriet, Calvin Stowe's wife, was more reflective, a born writer. Elizabeth remem-bered years later that it seemed natural to her that Harriet would write a book that would make her world famous and change society at the same time. Her copy of *Uncle Tom's Cabin*, which she sent east and got Harriet to autograph, was one of her most prized possessions. She gave it to her daughter Alice when years later Alice decided to become a teacher, and pointed out her favorite quote from the book, "Your little child is your only true democrat."

It was not only the people that Elizabeth met that had such a profound influence on her. It was the names she heard and the books she discovered. There was Rousseau's *Emile*; there were the works of Pestalozzi, the great Swiss educator, who taught children of the poor; and there were the works of Froebel, the German who created gardens for children, *kindergartens*. She was particularly struck by Froebel's ideas about the importance of play in learning. She had seen children learn through play and experimentation but hadn't articulated the importance of these processes for herself. When she returned to Turin she transcribed in a flowing and graceful hand a quote from Froebel and hung it up behind her desk. The quote read:

> Play is the first means of development of the human mind, its first effort to make acquaintance with the outward world, to collect original experiences from things and facts, and so exercise the powers of body and mind.[3]

Froebel and Pestalozzi weren't interesting only educationally. Elizabeth sensed in their work the same dream as the one that kept her teaching rather than raising a family of her own. The children could make democracy happen.

Elizabeth returned to Turin in the fall of 1838 with a renewed sense of the importance of her work. She told her students stories about what she had learned, organized a women's group to discuss issues of education pertaining to women, and became an even more ardent abolitionist.

Elizabeth wasn't the only educator in Turin who had encountered new ideas. John Clayton, the teacher at the church school, learned of the American Sunday School Movement and traveled to Philadelphia to meet John O. Crozer and spend time at his Baptist Sunday School. Crozer and other ministers were strong proponents of public support for education. However, they believed that public education should also be Christian education and that the United States should become a Christian democracy based as much upon the Bible as on the Consitution. They suspected deists like Horace Mann, the Stowes, and the Beechers who, though professed Christians, didn't believe in received authority and put too much emphasis on thinking things out for themselves.[4]

When John returned to Turin he convinced his congregation that their school should be a Christian public school and they applied for public funds, forcing Elizabeth for the first time to break her uneasy truce with John. The fight over God in the schools was fought in Turin and throughout the country in the 1830s, 1840s, and 1850s, and resulted in Turin, as in most places, in an uneasy compromise. John's school received some tuition reimbursement in exchange for conceding to Elizabeth's school the title Turin Common School.

During the late 1840s and the 1850s, Elizabeth devoted much of her time to the abolitionist cause, and when the Fugitive Slave Law was passed on September 18, 1850, she offered the basement of her house to the Underground Railroad. By then Elizabeth had ceased teaching and gotten married. It was sad for her to give up the school. She had been teaching since she was sixteen and informally even before that. But as she entered her thirties she realized that new things were stirring within her. Even though it was uncommon for a woman over thirty to marry, she wanted a child of her own, a family, and at that time it was considered inappropriate for married woman to teach. A widower, a friend of her brother's, proposed and she accepted. She had to give up her children to have a child. She also wanted to work with adults, to teach people about the impossbility of having slavery within a true democracy. She wanted to develop higher educational opportunities for women, and one time persuaded Catherine Beecher to come to Turin to talk to their women's group. Her school was taken over by one of her students who had attended a professional teachers college.

The late 1840s and the 1850s were a time of turmoil. The issue of slavery and division of the North and the South were becoming increasingly painful. After the abortive revolutions in Europe in 1848, many European educators and revolutionaries migrated to the United States, and many German-speaking ones settled in Ohio, where there already was a substantial German population. These forty-eighters carried many of Froebel's, Pestalozzi's, and Rousseau's ideas to the United States, and many people heard about kindergartens for the first time from them.

In 1851, kindergartens were banned in Prussia as being revolutionary. Froebel, an old man by this time, was heartbroken but dreamed of developing kindergartens in the United State, a place where the dream of democracy was still alive. Elizabeth remembered hearing Elizabeth Peabody, the sister-in-law of Horace Mann, a Froebelian and leading American educator, lecture on Froebel and was particularly struck by some of Froebel's last words. He said to his companion, the Countess von Bulow, "Now if people will not recognize and support my cause in my native land I will go to America, where a new life is freely unfolding itself and a new education of man will find a footing.[5]

The Civil War was a trauma. In Turin there were many southern sympathizers, and Elizabeth's educational ideas and her politics were lumped together as subversive. She was a staunch Unionist but saw beyond the issues of North versus South to more fundamental issues of economics. She had befriended one of the forty-eighters and learned of the works of Karl Marx. She strongly disagreed, felt he was too atheistic and violent. Yet there was a truth to his analysis she couldn't deny. Slavery was an economic issue in the South as well as a human one, and perhaps the economic explanation could account for the acceptance of slavery by many otherwise decent people. Marx confused and angered her because he called into question the fundamental importance she placed on education.

Elizabeth's daughter, Alice, a late and only child, was born just before the Civil War. She grew up during the misery of the war, and the confusion and demoralization that followed it. Her mother tried to protect her from many of the horrors, but it was impossible not to experience the physical and psychological scars the war left on its participants. Turin, divided during the war, had a particular need of a healing time, and Elizabeth decided to do something. There were so many problems that she decided to focus on those she knew best, those relating to the common schools.

The town experienced an influx of Blacks from the South whose education had to be provided for. There were also new migrations from Pennsylvania, New England, and Europe. By 1868 the potential student population was near 150, too large to be accommodated in a one-room school or the Christian School. If the community was to build a new school, there had to be some way to reconcile all the differences that existed in the community. Elizabeth, with the assistance of the teachers of both schools, convened a series of town forums on education, quite unaware of what she was opening up. On the first night parents from the fundamentalist school came in a large group. Some members of the business community attended, as well as several of the farmers from the surrounding area. A handful of parents from Elizabeth's former school also came. Only two Black adults came. They were friends of Elizabeth's and came more as a favor to her than out of their own conviction. The racism that was generated by the defeat of the South and the influx of Blacks led most Blacks in Turin to keep to themselves for safety.

Elizabeth was her usual romantic self. She believed people could solve problems, that one school could be created that would be excellent and satisfy the community. Her Black friends and her Marxist friend as well could have told her differently, but she wouldn't have listened anyway.

From the outset the meeting was dominated by representatives of the business community. They expressed concern about building a new school, when the community already had two school buildings and some informal arrangements for Blacks in community homes. After all, the population could decrease and leave an empty building. There were many arguments against a new building. However, an eloquent plea by both teachers almost convinced the businesspeople that it would be in the children's and the town's best interest to build a new school. Only . . . no one wanted to say the *only,* but at last, in a hesitant way, one of the farmers suggested that it would be possible to save money and solve a problem by giving one of the old schools to the local Blacks. With the exception of Elizabeth and her freinds, everyone was relieved. The town could have a school, Blacks would have a school. The only thing to be worked out was how progressives and fundamentalists could get along in the same building. As the fundamentalist teacher put it, "My students are quiet and orderly and they won't disturb anybody. The other students are the ones who talk and move around so much. If you can find a way for your students not to disturb mine we'll get along fine." The compromise reached created more problems than it solved. The Black community was relegated to an old school and the new school became increasingly fundamentalist. A third teacher was hired who was more fundamentalist than not. The two one-room schools were now four one-room schools, three physically attached and one separate. There was no unity of purpose or philosophy, and the White parents could choose which of the three classes they preferred. Each class was multigraded, and each teacher had control of a small budget and, within limits created by the parents, the power to teach as he or she chose.

Elizabeth's child, Alice, hated school and schools. There was altogether too much talk about schools and education around her house. She liked to read, to run with the boys, and to be left alone. She couldn't understand why her mother worried so much about what was happening in the school. To her, school was a place you tolerated for five hours a day and also a place where you occasionally learned something interesting. It wasn't until she was fourteen, in 1871, that school seemed more than a chore to her. For Christmas in 1871 one of her uncles gave her a copy of Louisa May Alcott's *Little Men.* He knew she loved *Little Women* and felt close to the wild tomboyish Jo, and supposed correctly that Alice would like to know what happened to Jo when she grew up.

"Jo became a teacher, that's what!" Alice told her mother. At first Alice was disappointed, but as the book unfolded it became clear that Jo's school was not like her school. There was an understanding of child life that she hadn't experienced in Turin. And there was a mixing of classes and a compassionate understanding of children in trouble that she had never experienced. She identified with Nat and his fiddle. She also wanted to know about Louisa May Alcott the writer and asked her mother, who seemed to know or know *about* everybody.

Elizabeth laughed a bit at the question. She knew of the Alcotts, not just Louisa May but the whole family. She took down a book to show Alice. It was Elizabeth Peabody's *Record of a School* published din 1835 in Boston. It was the story of the Temple School run by Bronson Alcott, Louisa May's father. Alice knew about Elizabeth Peabody, the kindergarten lady who had lectured in Turin. She was one of her mother's idols, the person responsible for introducing kindergartens into the United States and known for defending the rights and dignity of children.

Elizabeth explained to Alice that Bronson Alcott tried to create a school where boys and girls of all classes could go to school together and grow naturally and with love for each other in the world. He even took in a Black student at a time when there were hardly any other integrated schools in the country. That was in the 1830s, and people couldn't tolerate his ideas and principles. Also, he was a little strange and dogmatic. For many reasons, the school didn't last long, but Bronson's daughter Louisa May made it live on in *Little Men.* Jo, the wild one of *Little Women,* became what in the 1860s and 1870s was called a "modern teacher." She believed in child-centered learning, in collective work with children, and in learning though experimentation. She advocated what Henry Barnard (later the first United States commissioner of education) described in 1868 as education, as opposed to instruction:

> Instruction calls into exercise a sort of passive activity, a reception of facts and a perception of relations as presented. Education trains the pupil to discover relationships, and to make deductions from facts, and thus excites independent activity. Teachers and books instruct when they convey thoughts and explain processes; they educate in so far as they lead the pupil or reader to think for himself and to institute new processes. . . . Thus although instruction and education are inseparable, there may be much instruction where there is very little education, and very little instruction where there is much education. *Instruction is limited to what the teacher does; education is measured by what the pupil is rendered competent to perform.*[6]

As Alice got older she overcame her reluctance to imitate her mother and toyed with the idea of teaching. When she was eighteen, her mother, who was usually not so aggressive, gave her a book called *Reminiscences of Friedrich Froebel*, written by Baroness von Marenholz-Bulow and translated into English by Mary Mann, the second wife of Horace Mann and sister of Elizabeth Peabody. The book told of the baroness's relations with Froebel and described the magic of his kindergartens. Alice was particularly moved when Froebel was quoted as saying, "The kindergarten is the free republic of childhood." She remembered her mother's favorite quote form *Uncle Tom's Cabin*: "The child is the only true democrat." She found herself caught up in the romance of education. She volunteered to help out in the schools at Turin and after a while decided she could be more useful tutoring reading at the school in the Black community than at the one she attended.

Elizabeth, despite her age, kept up on things happening in education. She followed the work of Henry Barnard, subscribed to all the journals of modern education, and kept correspondence with dozens of educators throughout the country. She contributed to many journals, though no one in Turin, including her own daughter, would have suspected that she was highly regarded as an educational thinker. One experiment that she followed with particular interest took place in Quincy, Massachusetts, in 1873.

The school board of Quincy, Massachusetts, sensing that all was not right with the system, decided to conduct the annual school examinations in person. The results were disastrous. While the youngsters knew their rules of grammar thoroughly, they could not write an ordinary English letter. While they could read with facility from their textbooks, they were utterly confused by similar material from unfamiliar sources. And while they spelled speedily through the required word lists, the orthography of their letters was atrocious. The board left determined to make some changes, and after a canvass of likely candidates, elected Francis Wayland Parker as superintendent.[7]

Parker, known to everyone as Colonel Parker since his service in the Civil War, was a schoolteacher before the war. He began teaching in 1853 at the age of sixteen and worked with young people until the Civil War. After the war he taught in Dayton, Ohio, where he was the principal of the first normal training school (as teacher-training institutes were called) in the country. He got in trouble in Dayton for criticizing textbooks. He was attacked by the publishing companies, but he was a tough fighter and emerged as assistant superintendent in Dayton. In 1871, after his wife died unexpectedly, Parker left Dayton bereaved. Instead of going back to teaching, he went to Europe, following the same path as Calvin Stowe, Horace Mann, Henry Barnard, and other leading American educators. He met with Froebelians, visited Pestalozzi's school, and talked with educators throughout the Continent. Upon returning to the United States he was hired by the Quincy, Massachusetts, school board.

In Quincy, Colonel Parker made drastic changes:

> The set curriculum was abandoned, and with it the speller, the reader, the grammar, and the copybook. Children were started on simple words and sentences, rather than the alphabet learned by rote. In place of time-honored texts, magazines, newspapers, and materials devised by the teachers themselves were introduced into the classroom. Arithmetic was approached inductively, through objects rather than rules, while geography began with a series of trips over the local countryside. Drawing was added to encourage manual dexterity and individual expression. The emphasis throughout was on observing, describing , and understanding, and only when these abilities had begun to manifest themselves — among the faculty as well as the students — were more conventional studies introduced.

The program was an immediate success and attracted national attention as the "Quincy System." Teachers, school superintendents, and newspapermen descended on the schools in such numbers as to require restrictions to prevent interference with the daily work. . . . Parker himself decried the fuss, protesting that there was nothing at all novel about the Quincy approach. "I repeat," he wrote in his report on 1879, "that I am simply trying to apply well established principles of teaching, principles derived directly from the laws of the mind. The methods springing from them are found in the development of every child. They are used everywhere except in school. I have introduced no new principle, method, or detail. No experiments have been tried, and there is no peculiar 'Quincy System.'"[8]

Elizabeth was intrigued by Colonel Parker's work and felt that Parker's description of himself described her feelings about her own life and work perfectly:

I can say that all my life I have had a perfect passion for teaching school, never wavered in it in my life, and never desired to change. I never had anything outside offered me that had any real attraction to me, and I never decided to go outside the field—it was a sort of wonder to me that I did have such a love for it. I remember when I was teaching in the Grammar School in Piscataquog I had a small garden. Then we lived near the old home where I was born, and I had a bit of rocky, gravelly garden, that I used to tend and hoe, morning and night; beans and corn and so on. Always it seems to me when I was hoeing I was dreaming and thinking of school. I remember one day I was hoeing beans. I remember just where I stood when I said to myself, "Why do I love to teach school?" And then I looked around on the growing plants and said, "It is because I love to see things grow." If I should tell the secret of my life, it is the intense desire I have to see growth and improvement in all living things, and most of all human beings.[9]

Elizabeth read that quote often and dreamed of knowing more about how Parker and his coworkers did what she had been trying to do for years. Colonel Parker left Quincy in 1882 to become director of the Cook County Normal School in Chicago, to work with children and to train teachers. If only Alice were interested in becoming a teacher!

Alice had had enough of the volunteer life. She was considering marriage, considering going to normal school, considering many things since she passed twenty-five. When Elizabeth finally got the courage to tell Alice about the Cook County Normal School and the possibility of going to Chicago to study, Alice was ready. Chicago was a solution of sorts. It would give her two years to think and learn, to decide whether she wanted to stay in Turin to have a family, or teach, or both, since it was now possible. Alice had no problem getting into the Cook County Normal School and arrived in Chicago in the fall of 1883. Several letter she wrote to her financé, Ralph Burns, described her impressions:

Chicago, October 15, 1883

My Dear Ralph,

Your letter reached me a few days ago. I want to thank you for its great and kind support for my current adventure. Chicago is not a kind place for one used to the size and dimension of life in Turin. Without the kind assistance of Pastor Bennor and the generosity of the congregation, I would have abandoned this city and returned to my small and comfortable classroom.

Please give my warmest regards to your family and my parents, who should have received several letters during the last week. Give my special regards to my mother and inform her that in the next week I will have an interview with Colonel Parker. I am not sure whether to thank her for convincing me to travel so far from Turin or to beg her for permission to give up and return home.

Please think well of me. Yours faithfully and with warmest regards,

Alice

Chicago, October 29, 1883

My Dear Ralph,

It has been most encouraging having your letters come so often and so regularly. My interview with Colonel Parker has finally arrived and passed. I am very confused by what I have seen and what he has said and done.

Colonel Parker is a large man though it is genuinely difficult to gauge the size of him. He doesn't sit down and doesn't do just one thing at a time. During my brief interview, there were children coming to him with questions about every subject. There were visitors from New York, a journalist who had come to inspect the school, and several teachers undergoing training. I don't know if I can be at all like them and don't know how I'll manage the constant activity around here.

I simply do not understand what is happening at the school. Rose Thomas, one of the teachers, gave me a tour, but I cannot say what I have seen. Forgive my confusion. I must write to mother and ask her what to expect.

Your warm and confused friend,

Alice

Chicago, December 1, 1883

Dearest Ralph,

I don't know what is more remarkable, the public school or the course of study at the Cook County Normal School. Colonel Parker said in a talk to new students that a course of study must be flexible if he is to train flexible teachers. We are all to do manual labor, to study the history of education, and to learn how to teach reading and arithmetic without the use of textbooks or workbooks. Colonel Parker said that textbooks are the work of the devil and they shrivel minds.

Today I was introduced to printing, which I am to master. I have not seen a printing press before, much less used one. But learning to operate a press is part of my instruction in the teaching of reading. The press is used to print our reading lessons, which consist of our children's poems and stories as well as the remarkable writings on scientific observations they make in Mr. Jackman's class and upon class trips. The press is also used to prepare material for the *Chicago Normal School Envelope,* which is written by Colonel Parker and the rest of the staff. The *Envelopes* contain stories of the work at the school and I have learned much from them.

I am extremely busy these days and hope you will forgive me for not writing as often as in my time of confusion and loneliness. I still hold you in the same high regard and think of you often.

Your warm friend,
Alice

March 3, 1884

Dearest Ralph,

I believe I have seen a pattern to all the movement and activity here. The key to understanding Colonel Parker's work is to see that the children think for themselves, have a voice in what happens at the school, and, though they are cooperative and considerate, do not sit still waiting to be given an assignment. I have never been so tired working with young people and never so elated.

I am working on a unit on employment and workers' organizations in Chicago. We have studied the crafts unions and some cooperatives.

I have talked with a representative of the Knights of Labor who will visit the school. The class is planing a pageant depicting the history of Working People in America. The students in art are making posters and costumes. My reading class is writing the script and we will print it at the school. The woodworking class is making a speaker's platform and models of factories. I have never seen so much bustle. A visitor would think us possessed and disorganized, yet it all coheres about a theme so that one of our young carpenters could tell of labor history and our actors know just what our carpenters are up to.

All this is the more astonishing in that Colonel Parker is under constant attack from the *Chicago Tribune* and certain members of the Chicago school board. They simply do not or will not understand what we are doing. Occasionally I can see the Colonel's mustache twitch and imagine him to be trembling with rage. At times he walks the halls muttering "how long, how long," though he said at assembly yesterday, and we believe him, that someday people will understand our work for the children.

I look forward to resting and spending the summer being with you in Turin. Please share this with mother as I have no time to write. The Colonel insisted that I contribute my unit to the *Envelope,* and though I protested my inadequacy, he said that if one's work is too poor to bear the light of day, it is too poor to occupy the time of children. And seeing my hesitancy he added that the greatest courage is to male mistakes and grow through them. I don't know but that I might become a writer too.

With warmest reads I remain your friend,

Alice

Alice returned to Turin the summer of 1884 and finished her training at the Cook County Normal School the next year. In the summer of 1885 she married Ralph Burns. She was also fortunate enough to get a job at the Turin Common School, which kept on growing as Turin and the United States became industrialized. Alice's work was accepted. A modern America entering the twentieth century would need modern schools that stressed flexibility, invention, and the ability to adjust to the social demands of progress. The newspapers during the 1890s called the twentieth century "The Century of the Child"; it was also called the "American Century."

Progressives grew as industry grew. In Turin, attacks were mounted on fundamentalist education from two groups, not in the name of progress. One group felt that it was basic that schools prepare students to take their roles in a growing industrial world. The other group agreed that students should be prepared for industrial society, but added preparation for a socially progressive society. The former group consisted of many members of the business and farming communities as well as managers of the steel mill and the tool-and-die factory that had just opened outside of town. The latter consisted of some farmers, workers, and businesspeople, who ranged from Teddy Roosevelt Progressives to Eugene Debs socialists. Both groups agreed that fundamentalist education was inadequate for the twentieth century.

As one of the members of the Chamber of Commerce put it, "Children have to be prepared for change. Reading, writing, and arithmetic won't be enough in the new century. They must learn how to learn."

In that context Joseph Mayer Rice's indictment of the public schools published in 1893 was widely read and discussed.[10]

People were also concerned a few years later with Scott Nearing's analysis of the effects of a rigid minimal three-Rs curriculum:

> It is probable that the majority of children who enter American schools receive no more education than will enable them to read clumsily, to write badly, to spell wretchedly, and to do the simplest math problem (add, subtract, etc.) with difficulty. In any real sense of the word, they are neither educated nor cultured.[11]

Alice discussed education issues with her mother, Elizabeth, right up until Elizabeth passed away in 1894. They followed Joseph Mayer Rice's articles in *The Forum* and appreciated his defense of Colonel Parker. Yet Alice, more than her mother, sensed something lacking in "modern" education too. The late nineteenth century was substantially different from pre-Civil War in America. Many of the older books seemed stiff and outmoded. The math and science taught even in the "modern" schools were obsolete. Children of the twentieth century would have to deal with new needs of society, with engineering and mechanization, with increased mobility. How could education be useful in an industrial society and still be natural and humane? That was a major question that Alice and many of her contemporaries struggled with.

In 1896, two years after her mother's death, Alice decided to return to Chicago for renewal. She had taken a leave from teaching in 1895 when her first child, Phillip, was born and wasn't sure whether she had the energy to return to the classroom. Her aunt took care of the baby, and Ralph somewhat reluctantly let her go. Her old friend and teacher from the normal school, Rose Thomas, had a large house and gave Alice a room. During the time of Alice's stay in Chicago from spring 1896 to spring 1897, the following events were held at the University of Chicago campus: the annual institute of the Cook County Teachers; a meeting of the Illinois Society for Child Study; conferences on teaching English, mathematics, reading, the arts; a celebration of the 150th anniversary of the Birth of Pestalozzi; and most important for Alice, a series of public lectures on the science and art of teaching by Colonel Parker, and a seminar on education conducted by Professor John Dewey, who had arrived on Chicago in 1894.[12] Alice heard of Dewey from Rose, who first met him when he enrolled his children in Colonel Parker's school. Rose also attended Dewey's first seminar on education at the University of Chicago.

Colonel Parker's lectures were Alice's main source of renewal. His theory of concentration, which put the natural and human sciences at the center of the curriculum, even for the very young, confirmed what Alice had learned from her own work with Children. Language and math skills grew out of studying what was interesting. You didn't first teach discrete reading and math skills and then hope they would be applied. You began with a lively exploration of the world and made it clear to children how reading and number skills enriched that exploration. Colonel Parker's diagram of his theory became for Alice what the framed quote from Froebel was for her mother. She framed it and put it over the study desk she built for herself in her living room.

Alice realized in Chicago that she wanted to return to the classroom. Hearing about Pestalozzi and Horace Mann, celebrating their work, made her think of her mother's work and all the unfinished tasks in Turin, the deprived Black children, the children of factory workers, the Eastern European immigrant children who were arriving in greater numbers. There were old unsolved school problems and new ones resulting from immigration and industrial growth. Professor Dewey tried to address himself to these problems and to the philosophical base for educational action as well.

Dewey was in many ways the opposite of Colonel Parker. He was dry and a bit wry, given to rambling. Someone in his seminar said that he spoke the longest paragraphs in the world. However, his students recognized that, however involuted and complex his words were, they had weight and substance. Dewey in his early work tried to reconcile the free individual, the natural person, with the citizen in an industrial state. How can children be educated so that industry and progress serve the growth of all the people rather than merely profit a few? That was Dewey's challenge, and in 1897, toward the end of Alice's stay in Chicago, Dewey published *My Pedagogic Creed*, which became as important to Alice as *Uncle Tom's Cabin* was to her mother.

Upon returning to Turin, Alice shared Dewey's work with her friends and colleagues. She was particularly taken with the end of the *Pedagogic Creed*, where Dewey stated,

> I believe that education is a regulation of the process of coming to share in the social consciousness; and that the adjustment of individual activity on the basis of this social consciousness is the only sure method of social reconstruction.
>
> I believe that this connection has due regard for both the individualistic and socialistic ideals.[13]

"Due regard for both the individualistic and socialistic ideals." That was what Alice's goal in the classroom had been, was the legacy her mother had left her. Alice remembered the project she'd done at the normal school on working people in America, and planned a whole series of projects for her return to teaching. She would use Colonel Parker's idea of putting content at the core of the curriculum, but her content would be social, not geological or geographic. Ralph warned her that she might be asking for trouble. He wasn't so sure that Dewey wasn't a red, and besides, he didn't like Alice's partiality to Eugene Debs in politics. Alice went ahead, as did hundreds of other teachers, in developing the social content of the curriculum.

Her class of sixth-graders explored their community. (During the time of her absence, the school had reached a critical mass, and it had been decided to imitate some of the larger cities and group students by age, which was considered quite progressive at the time.) The students did voter surveys, talked to people in local businesses and in the factories. They visited poor families and spoke with a few pioneer social workers (friends of Alice's from Chicago, where they were trained by Jane Addams at Hull House). They wrote about what improvements were needed in the community, and became involved in a project to build a park in the immigrant section of town. They also read books about the kinds of things they were experiencing. Some of the parents didn't approve of Alice's methods, and there was some grumbling. Because of the reorganization of the school, everyone had to have their twelve-year-olds in Alice's class, and conflict was bound to develop. When parental choice was taken away by the school board, parental conflict increased. Alice was able to survive the grumbling and occasional hostility because no parents could ever say that their children didn't learn reading, spelling, and arithmetic. She practiced what she learned from Colonel Parker: Openness does not mean an abandonment of standards.

At the turn of the century Alice was a Deweyite, a socialist who did not believe in violent revolution but who did believe, as Dewey put it, that

> it is fatal for a democracy to permit the formation of fixed classes. Differences of wealth, the existence of large masses of unskilled laborers, contempt for work with the hands, inability to secure the trianing which enables one to forge ahead in life, all operate to produce classes and to widen the gulf between them.[14]

Not everybody who believed in progress and industrialization believed that schools should train students to create a socialist society, Many people in Turin who agreed with certain aspects of Dewey's pedagogic ideas disagreed with his social goals. One could believe in training students to think, in learning through doing and through involvement in community activities, in preparing students to respond to the varying and often unpredictable demands of a growing industrial society and international power, and still be a capitalist.

The people in Turin who were not Dewey socialists and yet wanted to modernize the schools called their plans for the school the Bessemer model of education. This model developed by analogy with the Bessemer process for making steel. Before Bessemer developed this process, steel was made by heating iron ore very carefully in order to eliminate impurities and at the same time keep in the right amount of carbon needed to produce a good grade of steel. This process required great skill and was quite unreliable. Bessemer developed a completely different way of making steel. The Bessemer process consisted of superheating the iron ore to drive out all the carbon and other impurities, then adding back to the melted-down ore just the right quantities of carbon and other substances needed to make high-quality steel. It was a simpler, more efficient, and predictable process.

The Besssemer process of education advocated by a number of people in Turin and other places throughout the country was to get rid of everything that didn't work in the schools and, if possible, begin all over again in a scientific way. Techniques, materials, and people were to be brought into school under scrutiny. Everything should be studied, and whatever didn't work should be eliminated. It was hoped that through this process schools would produce high-quality students just as the Bessemer process produced high-grade steel.

About this time, in the first decades of the twentieth century, the "science of education" was developing. IQ and achievement tests were being tried out for the first time on a fairly large scale. A number of educators at teacher training institutions (many of which were now colleges instead of normal schools) became involved in planning programs for local school districts. Often these educators (many of whom considered themselves scientific progressives) were not schoolteachers but trained psychologists and statisticians. They believed that the schools, especially in large districts, needed rational planning and scientific management. Many of the plans they made laid the groundwork for the development of nonteaching school bureaucracies.

In 1904, at the request of the local business community, the school board in Turin turned to the state teachers college for advice. A professor for the state university in Canton visited Turin and studied the situation, and recommended that the district hire a professional principal/superintendent, a trained educational expert who could develop a unified program for the community and train teachers in current methods. He also recommended that the school for Black students be closed, that Alice's school be enlarged, and that the children in the expanded plant be grouped by ability, with two classes in each grade. That way, he implied in his report to the school board, Blacks and immigrants could be separated from "native" children on a scientific basis.

Alice and her colleagues resented the new plans, as did many members of the community. The experts hadn't consulted them. A plan was drawn up without any local input, the gist of which was to put an outside expert in charge of the whole system. The teachers felt that, even though they had differing educational and political views, they had evolved ways of living together and making communal decisions about issues that affected the whole school. Now their power was taken away in the name of science, and they had no idea what would be imposed upon them. Alice, as chosen representative of the staff, spoke before a board meeting opposing the expert's recommendations. However, the business community's representatives were adamant that scientific planning was needed if schools were to serve changing social and economic conditions. The recommendations were accepted with the specific promise, insisted upon by the fundamentalists and the business community, that an Americanization program be instituted as soon as the new principal/superintendent took over.

Americanization was a major issue in the schools in the early twentieth century. In Turin the new mill and factory attracted workers who had recently come from Italy and eastern Europe. This new influx of peoples created problems for schools throughout the country. The immigrants did not speak English, and the teachers were not trained to work with students who couldn't understand them. The newcomers also had cultural habits that seemed strange to Turin's old-timers. They became "problems" and their children were "problems."

In New York City, for example, there were complaints about Irish and Italian students being unmanageable in the schools and lawless on the streets. Discipline and Americanization were thought to be solutions to these problems of ghetto schools. However, the students resisted. Angelo Patri, in his book *A Schoolmaster of the Great City*, described his first teaching experience in a public school in East Harlem in 1907. He was given fifty students, and he tried to use the strict methods he was trained to use. He discovered that "discipline, my great stronghold, had failed for I had come into contact with those who defied discipline."[15]

Patri had heard his "fellow teachers . . . talking about Education, the Science of Education and its principles. It appeared that there were men who could teach a man why he taught and how to do it. There was one thing I had learned and that was the insufficiency of my equipment as a teacher. Discipline, boss standard, was nerve taxing and not altogether productive."[16]

Patri went to Teachers College, Columbia, in 1907, just a few years after John Dewey had moved from the University of Chicago to Columbia. After Columbia, Patri returned to teaching with new principles and with a belief that

> unless a school enters deeply into the lives of the people, that school will not enter deeply into the lives of children or into the lives of teachers. Unless the school is the great democratic socializing agency, it is nothing at all.[17]

Patri put his progressive and scientific views on education into practice upon returning to teaching and, as principal of a junior high school, created a model of a progressive urban immigrant ghetto school.

Alice was to meet Angelo Patri in 1920 when he was the keynote speaker of the first meeting of the Progressive Education Association, which she joined as soon as she heard about it in 1919, the year it was founded. Before that she was a member of the National Education Association, which she joined in 1905 in order to keep in touch with developments in her profession. The first twenty years of the century were exciting ones in education. The work of Colonel Parker and others, as well as the ideas of John Dewey, seemed to be coming to fruition.

Alice was representative of this progressive movement and brought that perspective to the superintendent selection committee in Turin. Searching for an acceptable principal/superintendent was harder than anticipated. One criterion for the selection that quickly emerged from community debate was that the new administrator be able to deal with pressure and conflict. No single idea about what the basic role of the school should be was going to be accepted by all the citizens of Turin.

Despite the problems, the job was filled in 1905. There were many people coming out of teachers colleges with energy and new ideas at the turn of the century. The new superintendent was a kind of educator the community had not experienced before. Because of the number of divisions within the community, the board decided to choose someone who claimed to be neutral politically and scientific educationally. They chose John Dorfman, a person who had big city teaching experience, was a principal in a small city, and had done several semesters of graduate work at Teachers College, Columbia, with Edward Thorndike and his students, on the measurement of teacher effectiveness and pupil achievement.

Dorfman puzzled Alice. He considered himself an education progressive and supported her work. At the same time, he disassociated himself from progressive political ideas, which to Alice were the basis of progressive educational practice. He also worried her with his talk of testing and science. Yet she admitted that he helped the school overcome many educational and social problems. Dorfman arrived with a family, and his three children were immediately enrolled in the public schools. His wife became active in local civic organizations, and Dorfman worked hard, usually twelve hours a day, trying to reorganize and expand the school. He appeased the Deweyites by integrating community learning and activity methods in the curriculum. He quieted the fundamentalists by instituting achievement tests to prove that reading, writing, and arithmetic were learned. He persuaded the business community to raise a bond issue in order to build a new modern wing for the school. He seemed to incorporate all the different views in the community into the school, but there was a vague sense that by incorporating everything, nothing of substance was happening. The teachers were afraid to say much for fear he would find out about their internal conflicts. Alice was the only one who spoke out, and she got what she wanted for her class. Parents weren't sure about what to object to. They had no way to find out whether their children were learning more or less. The school was progressive and it wasn't; people were content and they weren't; and worrying about schooling became boring. For a while most people decided to leave the school in the hands of the principal, the professional, and turn to other community matters.

The advent of a principal/superintendent who considered himself a "professional" interested in the "science of education" had some interesting effects on the school. The principal made educational decisions without consulting people in the community. The school board's function was restricted for a while to voting confidence in the administrator's decisions. One of the teachers left and a new teacher, whom the principal had worked with before, was hired. Soon after the new teacher came in, the principal proposed a major reorganization of the school into an upper and lower division.

In 1910, after almost six years in Turin, Dorfman presented his comprehensive plan for the school. The new wing of the school was almost finished, and Dorfman felt secure enough to make his move. The boldness of the plan shocked even Alice. It was based on the Gary model, which was a plan for the reorganization of the Gary, Indiana, public schools that was being put into effect by William Wert, the superintendent in Gary.

The Gary Plan was an attempt to translate many of John Dewey's ideas into practice in an urban industrialized community. The school was to become the center of social, artistic, and intellectual life in the community. It would be open all day, every day of the year. This way it could provide adult education classes, especially English and citizenship classes, for the immigrant community. The school would also provide community services, have a nursery and health clinic, teach nutrition, and offer vocational education. The school itself would be organized into four centers: the shops, the labs and classrooms, the auditorium, and the playground. Students would rotate from one center to another on what came to be known as "the platoon system" or what we now call departmentalized learning. Teachers would become specialists, and instead of building new classrooms every time the student body increased, the utilization of the gym and auditorium by half the pupils at any one time would allow teaching to occur in a small number of classrooms. The program was designed to be progressive and economical.

Students would no longer have their own classrooms for the whole day, but would move from teacher to teacher. Instead of having their own desks, students would be given lockers in the hall. Perhaps the major lasting effects of the Gary Plan initiated in 1907 were these lockers and the departmental system, which now symbolize, ironically enough, dehumanizing aspects of school life.

When John Dorfman presented his version of the Gary Plan to the school board in Turin, everyone was shocked. Some people called it socialistic; others called it downright foolish. However, two aspects of the plan did make sense to the school board. One was the departmental system, which would save the school from building new classrooms even if the student population grew. The other was adult classes in English and citizenship. The board instructed Dorfman to proceed with those aspects of his plan, while in private they told him to forget about those notions of the school as a social and community center.

The teachers resisted the reorganization. They didn't want to become specialists, were afraid they didn't have the knowledge, and didn't want to teach five classes a day in one subject instead of one class in all subjects. They also felt that so much moving around from place to place would not be any good for the younger children. Alice was tempted by the program as she had wanted, for some time, to concentrate on developing some projects in writing and social studies. However, she too was cynical about such a drastic reorganization of the school. After many heated battles at faculty meetings, it was decided that the plan would be modified so that the upper division would adopt the platoon system and the lower division would remain in single classrooms. The cutoff between the divisions would be for twelve-year-olds or sixth-graders, who would be the oldest children to remain in self-contained classrooms.

Alice volunteered to be an English-social studies teacher under the condition that the school board send her to a training institute so that she could prepare herself for this new role. The principal and board agreed, and she spent the summer of 1911 at Teachers College, Columbia. As she told her family, it was good to have a new challenge when you were over fifty.

At Columbia she attended a seminar with Professor Dewey once again and took a class on curriculum-making with Professor William Hurd Kilpatrick. In that class Kilpatrick talked about the project method of organizing curriculum, too much, as if he had invented it, Alice thought, remembering her work at the Cook County Normal School. Nevertheless, she had to admit that Professor Kilpatrick had thought through ways to organize projects and that his ideas would be useful to her when she returned. She summarized her ideas of how a project developed and kept them pinned over the desk of her study at home:

> Projects arise from (1) A desire to understand the meaning and use of some fact, phenomenon, or experience. This leads to questions and problems. (2) A conviction that it is worthwhile and possible to secure an understanding of the thing in question. This causes one to work with an impelling interest. (3) The gathering from experience, books, and experiments of the needed information, and the application of this information to answer the question in hand.[18]

Alice always felt that the years from 1911 to 1917 were the most creative of her teaching career. She realized that there was some grumbling that the school's reorganization was reducing standards. But her teaching kept her alive. The reorganization put her in contact with immigrant and Black children more fully than she had ever been. She was appalled at how badly taught these children had been before they came to her, and she resolved to compensate for their educational neglect. During those years she thought about her mother a lot, and realized how close their commitment and work was even though it manifested itself in different forms.

World War I was a terrible experience for the people in Turin, as for the rest of the nation. There were two military drafts, a White draft and a Colored draft, and the segregation that existed in the services during the war broke down the fragile bonds that were developing between the Black and White communities. There were fights between the German immigrant community and the Anglo-Saxon community. People often took sides on the basis of national origin, and Alice saw all this in the schools, children fighting or refusing to associate with other groups of children. And the Russian Revolution led to a larger scale of red fear and red hating than she had experienced. People treated her with suspicion, as she had been a member of the Socialist party. During the last years of her teaching career, from 1919 to 1925, Alice spent most of her time trying to heal the old wounds the war had exacerbated. She also became more active in the National Education Association and the Progressive Education Association. In 1921, when the NEA created a delegate assembly, Alice became an Ohio delegate, and in 1923, at the annual meeting of the delegate assembly, which was held in Oakland, California, Alice presented a paper on how to use the project method to help students deal with cultural and racial differences.

At that meeting Alice heard several things that distressed her and reminded her how far folks were from achieving her mother's goal of excellent schools for all the children of all the people. She didn't consider herself much of a radical, but she worried that sensible progressive change would be crushed by purges within the education profession. She knew she was one of the anarchists being referred to in the address by James Fisk, chairman of the Americanism Commission of the American Legion, who warned the delegates about anarchists, socialists, and all other progressives.

Alice found the talk by Ellwood Cubberly, dean of the School of Education of Stanford University, to be particularly interesting. He articulated the problems she had been experiencing and came up with a program she thought was somewhat helpful:

> The six most important items in any forward-looking American school program, covering at least the next decade of work and service, are: (1) A comprehensive educational program to aid in the assimilation of the foreign-born we have among us; (2) the general provision of a good system of health and development education; (3) such a reorganization of our school curricula as will adapt to our school better to new conditions and needs on our National life; (4) the reorganization and redirection of rural education; (5) a much more general equalization of both the advantages and the burdens of education than we now enjoy; and (6) provision for the placing of an adequately educated and an adequately trained teacher in every classroom in the United States. Five of these six are at the bottom economic problems in that the necessary additional funds must be provided by our people before much can be done by educational workers to give effect to the proposals; only one — that of curricula reorganization — is primarily an educational problem. All of the six are primarily National in scope and importance, and call for National cooperation in their solution. In closing, let me add one more, and one which may easily become the major problem of them all.[19]

That last problem, which underlined the rest, was the absence of strong federal funding for education. The main theme of the convention in 1923 and over the next decade was the need for a strong Department of Education to equalize state funding for education so that the poor states would be able to spend as much on schools as rich states, and to provide funds for educational research.

Alice had mixed feelings about these issues. In Ohio there was a strong tradition of local control of schools, and Turin was no exception. She worried about whether Turin could solve its unique problems if there was strong federal control. Alice was even more distressed by what she saw as an increasing dominance of the National Education Association by university-based researchers. She had to exert considerable self-control throughout the speech by Charles Judd, who was the current director of the School of Education at the University of Chicago,

Colonel Parker rest in peace. She made notes on his remarks, quoting them whenever she talked to classroom teachers, trying to remind them of the importance of using classroom knowledge rather than bowing to demands imposed by "experts" who knew nothing about teaching. Her favorite quote was:

> My plea to this Association is that it make itself the center for the promotion of the one type of control that can find a permanent home on this continent—namely, control through research.[20]

After reading this last quote Alice would tell the teachers that what she had learned in her career was that educational problems were, at bottom, not academic research questions but issues of the heart and the will. That was the problem with her principal, John Dorfman, and with other administrators. They had research solutions that usually didn't work because they ignored the social and human context of learning.

Alice retired in 1925, and her two children didn't follow her into teaching. Her son, Phillip, became a dentist. He remained in Turin, taking a layman's interest in the schools, and during the thirties became a school board member. Her daughter, Elizabeth Ann, went to the University of Chicago School of Education at her mother's suggestion but transferred into the Department of Sociology. After college she moved to New York and received an M.A. in social work from Columbia. She remained in New York, working at the Henry Street Settlement House.

The main educational issue in Turin after the First World War was consolidation. The town was growing. It annexed two small unincorporated townships on its borders, and with that, the size of the school district almost doubled.

John Dorfman led the fight to build a new comprehensive high school and to turn the Turin school and the two schools from the newly annexed town into elementary schools. The fight for consolidation was supported by a coalition of businesspeople, progressives, and labor leaders who were trying to organize some of the local workers. They believed the high school would provide a better opportunity for students to acquire the range of skills needed to deal with the modern world. A science lab, special math and English teachers, an athletic program, a machine shop, and a printing program all seemed possible with consolidation.

Opposition to consolidation came from people who feared loss of local control. They argued that a big district would take the power of taxation out of their hands. It would make it harder for the school to be accountable to the various segments of the community. It would lead to a deterioration in basic skills and a general lowering of standards. Dorfman countered this argument by showing people a battery of newly developed achievement tests. He explained how the use of tests during the war had led to the refinement of the science of testing and assured the community that, with the use of an extensive testing program, students' progress could be monitored and standards maintained. None of the school board members or community leaders knew much about this new science of education, but accepted on faith that science made as dramatic a contribution to education as it did to technology and business. Consolidation passed, and John Dorfman became the first superintendent of the Turin Unified School District.

The new principal of the common school (now called the Turin Grammar School) was chosen by the superintendent and the enlarged unified school district. There was considerable grumbling in town about outsiders choosing their principal and rumors about his being a Communist and having a perverted sex life. The Russian Revolution and bohemian life in Greenwich Village were in the news those days, and there were constant allusions to progressives' being Communists or libertines. Of course, there were socialist progressive educators, child-centered progressives, and scientific progressives like the former principal/superintendent. There were probably some progressives who were Communists and some who had complicated sex lives. However, the progressive-education movement was not unified, though through John Dewey's name and the leadership he provided, it gave the impression of unity from without. From within, progressives battled other progressives, sometimes with greater energy than they expended on putting their ideas into practice.

The new principal in Turin was neither Communist nor libertarian. He was an energetic man in his late fifties who loved working with students. He is remembered by old-timers these days as a wonderful man who created an administrative mess. The principal's interest was in the "project method," and he worked with the teachers and older students to develop a project curriculum for the whole school. He even persuaded Alice to com out of retirement and train the teachers in the project method. Alice and Walter Johnson became close friends and worked together until Alice died of emphysema in 1933.

The curriculum of the Turin Grammar School was reorganized so that subject areas were replaced by projects, an idea John Dorfman supported but couldn't effect when he was principal. Now that he was superintendent he could provide the support for Walter Johnson to do it, and he even made Alive part-time curriculum supervisor.

Each project was meant to relate to life in the community and to subjects that interested the students. The projects were to integrate reading, writing, math, science, the arts, and social studies. They were not to be chosen at random but in such a way that what the skills students had to learn would be carefully integrated into project study. In getting approval to develop a project curriculum for the Turin Grammar School and helping the other grammar schools develop project curricula as well, Dorfman had the following quote entered into the school board's resolution approving the project as the basic component of the school program:

> If the project is to be made the basis of the curriculum, it is necessary for the teacher to decide as scientifically as possible what principles and processes should be mastered by the student and then to select not single projects but projects so arranged that selection of projects is made possible with the certainty that all essential facts, processes, and principles will be covered.[21]

Some of the projects students studied in Turin were:

EARLY GRADES (K to 1, 2)

1. planning, building, and planting a student-run vegetable garden;
2. studying the post office and setting up a student post office in the school;
3. studying and visiting the steel mill and the tool-and-die factory;
4. studying health and visiting and helping the town doctors and nurse.

UPPER GRADES (3 to 6)

1. collecting stamps and doing research on the places the stamps came from;
2. studying machinery and building a small electric go-cart;

3. from ranch to table: studying the flow of food from growing and raising to processing and marketing, visiting wholesalers, ranchers, farmers, and retail stores.

These projects represent just a few of those developed in Turin and throughout the country. The ultimate goal was to articulate them onto a comprehensive curriculum over the years.

There were parents and teachers in Turin who were angry at having the project method forced into the school. They felt it represented a neglect of the three Rs, and they didn't trust the test results produced by the superintendent to support his claim that skills were mastered best through developing interesting content. They were also angry about questions children were dealing with in school. There was no place, they claimed, for students raising social issues or questioning authority on the schools. Many teachers resisted all of Dorfman's innovations, and they had strong community support.

The depression hit Turin in the middle of the project method. There were major catastrophes in town. Money for the school was cut, some teachers had to leave. There were temporary panic and resentment from the more conservative members of the community. All these modern methods were worthless in a world of no jobs. The school should stick to reading, writing, and arithmetic, should not try to do so much. A new school board put pressure on the superintendent to cut programs, to eliminate anything that could be considered a frill. The principal's response was that his program was basic, that he didn't allow frills in his district. there were endless debates in barbershops, factories, and kitchens about what was basic in the society. The situation worsened until, in 1932, Roosevelt was elected with a mandate to give people a New Deal, to change society so all the people would have a good deal. There was grumbling among some people about socialism and communism, about loss of community control and federal interference in local affairs and business. But most people felt hope and believed that through planning, another 1929 could be avoided. The high school worked with the Civilian Conservation Corps; the grammar schools in the district continued to develop projects with increasingly social content. How can we help the community? was a theme worked into many of the projects. Helping out was basic. All the skills were taught in order to help rebuild the society.

Ever since he had been appointed principal of the Turin Grammar School, Walter Johnson had been vowing to spend part of his day teaching his favorite subject, American history. Alice kidded him about that dream. She told him that he'd never get around to teaching again. He took it in a good-natured way, but it depressed him. He loved to teach, and being a principal, though it had rewards, had none of the excitement of teaching for him. A few years after Alice died he decided to teach history to the upper grade of his school, "for Alice," as he said to his staff. He requested and got approval to buy a new social studies curriculum developed by Harold Rugg entitled *Man and His Changing Society*, and tested the curriculum in the schools himself. The curriculum was designed to assist students in thinking about different social systems, in analyzing social problems and considering alternate ways of solving them. At that time thousands of sets of the books were being used throughout the country.

Rugg's books tried to look at history from the perspective of working people. They tried to analyze problems associated with developing democracy in the United States. For example, in dealing with the making of the Constitution, Rugg analyzed the class and interests of the members of the Constitutional Convention and summarized the making of the United States Constitution in this way:

THE CONVENTION SET UP A GOVERNMENT BY
WHICH CHANGES WERE MADE DIFFICULT

The Fathers of the Constitution feared "too much democracy." They were afraid of what the majority of people, who did not possess property, would do to the minority, who did. They were afraid of what they regarded as the ignorance and rashness of the lower classes.

The spoken and written words of the men in the Convention show very clearly that they regarded democracy as a dangerous thing. Gerry, for example, said that the unsettled condition of the country "came from the excess of democracy."

Randolph used almost the same words, pointing out that the bad times were due to "the turbulence and follies of democracy." Another delegate, during the debate over the qualifications for Senator, maintained that the Senate should be made up of wealthy men "to keep down the turbulence of democracy."

Even Madison wanted to protect the small class of well-to-do people against the majority, that is, against the common people. In one of his writings he said:

"It is of great importance in a republic not only to guard the society against the oppression of its rulers, but to guard one part of society against the injustice of the other part. Different interests necessarily exist in different classes of citizens. If a majority be united by a common interest the rights of the minority will be insecure."

Alexander Hamilton wanted Senators to serve for life. He said:

"All communities divide themselves into the few and the many. The first are the rich and the well-born, the other, the mass of the people. . . are turbulent and changing; they seldom judge or determine right. Give, therefore, to the first class a distinct permanent share in the government. They will check the unsteadiness of the second, and as they cannot receive any advantage by change, they, therefore, will ever maintain good government."

Thus it was that the fathers wished to guard against the dangers of too much democracy. How did they do it?[22]

The Rugg texts were accompanied by workbooks encouraging students to study their own community and to analyze current political and social events for themselves. The texts were published in the context of the depression, when raising issues about the quality and purpose of the United States was natural. How could a society with such hope collapse so suddenly? And was the collapse sudden, or just the culmination of a long process of growth and the accumulation of wealth without regard for all the people or for the creation of a sensible, self-renewing future?

These arguments focused on the schools in 1940, when the National Association of Manufacturers announced that it would investigate school textbooks that were supporting communism and undermining the American way of life. The NAM joined the American Legion and a coalition of conservative organizations called the American Coalition. They claimed that the specter of collectivism was sneaking into the schools and that they had to be "sentinels" to protect capitalist America. The target these groups selected for their most violent attacks were the Rugg textbooks, which raised questions about social systems but meticulously avoided telling students what to think. In September 1940, the *American Legion Magazine* published an article entitled "Treason in the Textbooks" by O. K. Armstrong, which contained a strong attack on the Rugg textbooks.

Turin was not immune from the attacks on Rugg's texts. The county office of the American Legion as well as some business organizations banded together to eliminate from the Turin school not merely the textbooks but Walter Johnson as well. Johnson defended his use of the books and cited a study by leading historians from Harvard and Dartmouth that affirmed that the texts did not distort the primary documents of United States history in any way. He had depended upon this study to quiet this opposition, but it worked no better than the study of Colonel Parker's school had fifty years before. The opposition was political, not "scientific." The battle was won in the name of patriotism, fundamentalism, and, as one school board member said, "back to the basics." Walter Johnson resigned in early 1941. His resignation was accepted by the school board with only one dissenting vote, that of Dr. Phillip Burns, Alice's son.

Reaction to Walter Johnson's resignation was blunted by the onset of World War II, and for five years education went into the deep freeze. After the war the school grew at a phenomenal rate. Turin Grammar School doubled in size to about 300 students. The high school was up to 1,500 by 1950. Educationally, things were mixed. There was still some project teaching going on. A few classes were run by teachers of the fundamentalist persuasion. There were some teachers of who "taught by the book," meaning the teachers manual and the curriculum guides that came from the state board of education. The reading programs in the primary grades were indicative of the dispirited condition of the school. There was one teacher who taught strict phonics and swore by the book *Why Johnny Can't Read.* There was another one who taught by the look-and-see method and still used project learning. A third primary teacher used basal readers and workbooks. They never talked to each other about children or learning, and managed to get along without overt disagreement. The latest principal considered himself a manager, not an educator. Each teacher could do what he or she wanted as long as there was no trouble. The problem wasn't education so much as space and numbers.

The principal also knew what had happened in Pasadena in 1951, where the school board, using tactics similar to those that chased the Rugg text and the former superintendent out of Turin in the forties, ousted all the progressives in the district, from the superintendent on down. Anyone's job could be threatened during that time when innovation, progressivism, and communism were swept into one category.

During the early 1950s the principal's job was to keep things quiet and not allow the unpleasantness associated with the departure of the former principal to recur. The new man managed well and was supported by a large new middle class that developed during the postwar economic boom. They wanted an efficient school that would pass students on so that they could eventually get into the newly expanded state college system.

Concern about the nature and quality of education became a national issue again only after the Russians launched *Sputnik* in 1957, and there was a great outcry that our schools were the reason we had fallen behind in science and technology. The effect of *Sputnik* was to focus educational concern on the development of excellence, particularly in the areas of science and technology. For many people in power, the basic task of public education shifted from providing education for all children to the creation of a technocratic elite that would make us competitive with Russia. Hard thinking, learning to deal with abstractions, and technical training became skills that were considered basic to the survival of our society. Ironically, many of these skills were precisely those advocated by the progressives during the 1920s and 1930s.

The boredom and uniformity of school as well as the lowering of standards associated with the life-adjustment philosophy current at the time were considered the culprits. The adjustment philosophy was the result of an enormous growth in the use of psychology in education. Psychologists in the school were concerned with how students felt, with family problems, and with how students adapted to the social world of the school. They didn't worry much about math, science, reading—the so-called hard skills. The psychologists also pried into personal matters too much for the taste of some parents. The presumed lowering of standards and invasion of privacy caused by the adjustment philosophy led many parents in the late 1950s reluctantly to enroll their children in private schools.

This reluctance was expressed by John Keats, a professional writer and critic of the schools, who explained why he took his own children out of the public schools and put them in an expensive and, according to him, excellent private school during the late 1950s:

> We think continually of those whom we have left behind; . . . of children whose potentialities will never be realized by a school system which puts conformity ahead of accomplishment, which substitutes techniques for understanding, which underestimates children's desire and ability to do hard mental work and which . . . defrauds our youth of their right to a decent education while pretending to adjust them to life.[23]

One of the students left behind in the public schools was Ralph Stokes Burns, son of Phillip Burns, grandson of Alice Burns, and a great-grandson of Elizabeth Stokes. The Burneses refused to abandon the public school even in the negative climate of the 1950s. They explained the importance of public education as best they could to their children, and were delighted when a few years later the new president, John F. Kennedy, was able to get the Elementary and Secondary Education Act passed. After some dry years, the new president, whom the Burnses enthusiastically supported, managed to get the federal government to reaffirm support of the common schools. As part of this support, as well as in response to *Sputnik*, Kennedy also established an Office of Science and Technology at the Executive Office of the White House. That office convened a series of meetings of physicists, mathematicians, biologists, chemists, and other scientists, and set them to work on what later became the New Math, the New Biology, the New Physics. These curricula used many "learning by doing" principles, and had many hands-on activities. But what chiefly characterized them was a systematic approach to science based on current thinking and problem solving.

The principal in Turin was quick to adopt the New Science and New Math programs. He figured they were neutral enough to keep him out of trouble, nothing like the Rugg curriculum. When the material arrived at the school, there was excitement at first and then bewilderment. Only one of the teachers felt comfortable with math and science, and even she had trouble understanding how the new material related to children. The teachers received elegant, beautifully packaged, scientifically sound material that ignored their teaching styles, the organization and structure of their classrooms, and the nature of children. The teachers tried to use what little they understood of the materials, but they complained they didn't have enough time to teach the new program as well as all the other things expected of them.

The first- and second-grade teachers' complaints were similar to the ones voiced by other teachers. They felt that teaching basic addition and subtraction was done quite well at the school, and they didn't understand why they were expected to teach the associative and distributive rules of arithmetic—a+b=b+a and a+(b+c) = (a+b)+c—before getting to simple adding and subtracting. To the university professors who designed the New Math programs it made sense to teach these rules before simple addition and subtraction, as these principles were basic principles of algebra, group theory, and other fundamental areas in mathematics. Mathematically specific arithmetic examples could logically be derived from these and other simple principles. However, to the teachers, these principles baffled them and confused the children. For the most part, the teachers half-heartedly tried to teach these rules, but, with the tacit consent of the administrators, abandoned these attempts and returned to their old ways of teaching arithmetic through drill and practice.

People in the community reacted to the new material in different ways. Some people, especially those with college degrees or with a desire to have their children become scientists or engineers, were delighted. Others were upset over the de-emphasis of literature, poetry, theater, and the arts. A few kept up the cry of unwarranted government intervention, which had been part of the whole history of public schools in Turin. There was also a concern that drill and memorization were being ignored with all these fancy "modern" ideas. The most common complaint was that the material was so different that you could no longer help your children with their homework.

The sixties and the Civil Rights movement took most people in Turin by surprise. They had conveniently forgotten that the Black members of the community had been struggling to realize their share in the American dream for over 100 years. However, the Burnses were aware of the problems that existed in the school and in the economy. Alice's legacy wouldn't let them forget, and Phillip and his wife, Susan, passed on that sense of decency to their children. In the summer of 1964, during his junior year at the University of Michigan in Ann Arbor, Robert Stokes Burns went to Mississippi with many other Whites to support Black people's struggle for decency and justice. On returning from the Mississippi Freedom Summer, Robert decided that he had to become more involved. One summer wasn't enough. You had to build for the future, and the only way to do that was to reach the children. Why not teach and build democracy through the children? Robert chose the way of his grandmother and great-grandmother but didn't know it.

When he graduated from Michigan in 1965, Robert decided to get a teaching credential. Things were stirring again. There were Freedom Schools across the South, school boycotts in the cities. The March on Washington called for people to take a pledge, to commit themselves once again to the unfinished task of creating a democratic society. The open classroom was in the air, schools for democracy 1960s style. Robert took a job teaching in the Hough section of Cleveland. His students were mostly Black, all miseducated. After several years he began to discover respectful, creative ways to reach his students, ways confirmed in books like *How Children Learn, The Open Classroom,* and *The Lives of Children.* These books, combined with the analysis of the schools presented in *Death at an Early Age, The Way It Spozed to Be, 36 Children,* and *How Children Fail,* convinced Robert that he was part of a new movement that could change society through the schools. He was part of a movement, but not a new one. Once again the democratic impulse surfaced in public education, cut off from its roots in the common school movement, but with the same values and goals.

Robert met Joanna Berg in Hough. She was teaching third grade, and he was the new sixth-grade teacher. They struggled together to undo their student's bitterness about schools, to reach people in the community, and finally, as they felt they were about to succeed, were fired when the parents they worked with lost a major battle with the school district's central administration.

After seven years in Cleveland, Robert asked Joanna if she was willing to go with him to Turin, his hometown, and settle for a while, and take some rest and recreation. Robert had been offered a job teaching sixth grade by a friend of his family who was on the school board—and there was also talk of an opening teaching English at the high school, which Joanna might be interested in. He admitted to her that the offer was tempting, that he was tired of the struggle, that the songs didn't move him anymore, that there was no fun opposing the war or fighting poverty even though he felt obliged to do it. One night he even confessed that he wanted a child, wanted to be married and to work at being an excellent teacher. So much of their life had been consumed with being in opposition that neither of them felt they had enough time to do what they loved: working with young people. It was difficult for Joanna to admit that she too was fed up with the struggle, but she couldn't keep it from Robert. They knew each other too well to have any but small secrets.

Being tired and wanting to live quietly and do one's work well seemed like a moral failing, a betrayal of their friends as well as of their deepest beliefs. Yet they were tired, they wanted the adventure of having a child, and were afraid that since they were both over thirty it might soon be too late. They decided to try Turin for six months, and stayed.

During the seventies, Robert and Joanna taught quietly and effectively in Turin. Their values didn't change, but their style was low-keyed. In 1979, however, it was rumored that Robert was targeted by the Moral Majority as a dangerous influence on children who had be removed from his job. A petition was circulated in the community to have him fired for "inappropriate use of materials and inadequate discipline." It also called for a return to "old" teaching methods—drill, strict discipline, and rote learning.

Petitions to the school board are common in Turin. It's part of the Ohio tradition of strong local control of schools. There are usually several petitions circulating the community at any given time. Some deal with removing a textbook that a particular sect or group in the community finds offensive, others have to do with the elimination of electives, the addition of another school bus, the celebration of a new holiday, or the addition of compulsory prayers. They are mostly procedural in content and rarely name individual teachers or administrators. That was the most surprising aspect of the petition against Robert. It not only named him but was specific about bringing him to a personnel session and having him fired.

Robert and Joanna tried not to worry about the petition until they had more information, but it kept coming up. Robert hadn't done anything differently this year, none of his students' parents was complaining, what wasn't he seeing? Sure, every once in a while he raised criticisms of some of the things going on in the school, but only at formal meetings dealing with educational issues. Maybe some people didn't like his teaching about the Civil Rights movement or teaching his students about ecology and the need for simple living and self-sufficiency. Maybe they were upset by his giving the students lots of choices and control over their program, but parents didn't have to send their children to his class. In fact, over the last four years a tacit arrangement developed where parents who wanted a very structured program with an emphasis on drill and memorization requested Jim Bagley's class, and those who wanted something more open and content-oriented chose his.

Robert's parents knew all about the petition. It was circulated by some of their friends and, as his father tried to explain, wasn't meant as a personal attack on Robert. His class and his way of teaching were symbolic of changes taking place in Turin that were upsetting many of the older people. They didn't understand the ideas of many of the younger parents. In their minds solar energy, the smell of the natural-food store, opposition to nuclear power, and children without discipline were all threats to their way of life. They wanted all classes in the school to be alike and didn't like the way Robert went about teaching, not, his father admitted, that they really knew what Robert was doing or ever bothered to ask him or visit his classroom. The petition was part of a broader effort in the community and the state to ensure conservative domination of public institutions. The petition was aimed at Robert's activities as a citizen, not at his teaching.

"How should I fight back?" That was Robert's sole thought, how to protect what he had carefully built over ten years.

"How should I fight back?"

His father, who was an amazingly energetic and coherent eighty-four, answered in a way that surprised him:

"Your grandmother Burns would have known."

Robert never knew his grandmother; she had died before he was born.

"What do you mean?"

"We never talked much about Alice. She embarrassed us during her last days. Her mind wasn't here. All of her friends were dead. There's a lot of her in you. Maybe you need to know something about her now."

Robert was getting impatient. He had to develop a strategy, not learn about family history. His father could see his impatience but nevertheless persisted and took out a box of letters and clippings.

"Your grandmother, my mother, was a teacher and a troublemaker. Some of these things of hers might be of use to you."

That was how Robert and Joanna got Alice's letters and began to learn about her and Colonel Parker and John Dewey, about her mother Elizabeth, and about the fact that they were part of a nurturing tradition as old as our nation.

Robert's petition never came to a hearing. He had more friends, and his ideas had more advocates, than he imagined. What emerged from the petition were a series of community forums concentrating on what the common schools in Turin should be in the future.

Once again in Turin as in many other places, urban, rural, and suburban, the schools are the center of community conflict and the struggle to make democracy a lived reality in the United States.

CONCLUDING THOUGHTS

I ended my story here, in the late 1980s. Robert and Joanna are left to continue their efforts into the present and future while they turn to the past for inspiration. That chord in the story is essential. All of us—educators, parents, and concerned community members—need to look back as well as plan ahead. We are part of a continuing struggle and can learn from our past, from the works of Colonel Parker, Frederick Douglass, Elizabeth Peabody, John Dewey, and the dozens of others who have written elegantly of their struggles to make democratic education work. Some of their writings may sound dated, but much of it is inspiring as well as useful for our daily practice and our understanding of how to make education work for all children.

When I began teaching in the early 1960s, there was no progressive tradition for me to turn to, as far as I knew. I attended Teachers College, Columbia, in 1961 and found it dated and boring. Since I had not majored in education or read widely in the literature of schooling before beginning my teaching career, my work was not grounded in any theory of learning. What I discovered as a teacher emerged from daily contact with my students and with other teachers who were passionately involved in helping their students learn. Years later I learned that most of what I did was not new, but part of a progressive tradition with a long and proud history that is not taught in most teacher education classes. I believe my work would have been more effective had I known and studied this tradition, and I urge others to do this.

It helps to know that one is part of an important historic struggle during these embattled times. This knowledge can be a major source of strength and inspiration now, in the 1990s, when public education is under siege. For those of us who care about what at the turn of the twentieth century was called "the education of all of the children of all of the people," it is useful to surround ourselves with the spirit, creativity, and energy of past struggles. Studying our past is not an academic matter. It is a question of reaching back to the sources of our vitality and applying what we can learn from history to present struggles to keep democratic education alive.

These days the very enterprise of public education is threatened by right-wing and corporate attacks that threaten to either privatize public education or create a system of vouchers that would serve the well-off and punish the poor. Technological innovations demand a revision of what should be taught and how schools should be organized. The massive failure of urban public school systems has led to despair and thoughts of turning over schools to private enterprise or making them into minimum-security prisons. In addition, educators have to contend with a large Fundamentalist Christian movement that advocates "moral" books, censorship, and the insinuation of Christian fundamentalist ideology into the public arena.

Fortunately these negatives are counterbalanced somewhat by a number of wonderful efforts at school restructuring throughout the country. These range from the New Visions attempt to create new, community partnership high schools in the New York City public schools to the massive decentralization of the Chicago schools and the consequent restructuring of the whole system. New curriculum material, much of it created by progressive teachers, deals with racism, sexism, and homophobia. New multicultural and gender-fair textbooks have been created and widely distributed. Hundreds of other attempts to sustain the struggle for democratic schooling are under way throughout the nation. From a historical perspective, the struggle for democracy is once again fully engaged in the arena of public education.

I am, and have been, and continue to be committed to the struggles described in my story, *Education in Turin*. At the base of all these struggles are two driving ideas. The first is that passionate concern for justice is the core of all decent education. The second is that, no matter what current conditions seem to indicate, there is no child, no person, who cannot learn and grow through the caring and generous efforts of others.

NOTES

1. Franklin, *Proposals Relating to the Education of Youth in Pennsylvania* (1749), unpaged.
2. Stowe, *The Report on Elementary Public Instruction in Europe* (1837), p. 2.
3. Von Marenholz-Bulow, *Reminiscences of Friedrich Froebel* (1877), p. 67.
4. Wallace, *Rockdale* (1978). A marvelous account of the growth of an American village in the early Industrial Revolution. The author describes the book as "an account of the coming of the machines, the making of a new way of life in the mill hamlets, the triumph of evangelical capitalists over socialists and infidels, and the transformation of the workers into Christian soldiers in a cotton manufacturing district in Pennsylvania in the years before and during the Civil War."
5. Von Marenholz-Bulow, *Reminscences*, p. 200.
6. *First Century of National Existence: The United States as They Were and Are* (1872), p. 384.
7. Cremin, *The Transformation of the School* (1961), p. 129.
8. Ibid., pp. 129–30.
9. Parker, *Talks on Pedagogics* (1894).
10. Rice, *The Public School System of the United States* (1893).
11. Nearing, *The New Education* (1915), p. 18.
12. McCaul, "Dewey's Chicago," *The School Review* (Summer 1959), pp. 258–81.
13. Dewey, *My Pedagogic Creed* (1897), p. 16.
14. Dewey and Dewey, *Schools of Tomorrow* (1915), p. 313.
15. Patri, *A Schoolmaster of the Great City* (1923), p. 9.
16. Ibid., p. 13.
17. Ibid., p. 211.
18. This quotation appeared in Woodhull, "The Aims and Methods of Science Teaching," *General Science Quarterly*, vol. 2 (November 1917), p. 249. I attributed it to Alice for the sake of my story.
19. Proceedings of the NEA meeting in Oakland, California (1923), pp. 180.
20. Ibid., pp. 168.
21. Charters, *Journal of Home Economics*, vol. 10 (March 1918), p. 117.
22. Rugg, *America's March Toward Democracy* (1937). The Rugg textbook controversy was the subject of an entire issue of *Propaganda Analysis*, vol. 4, no. 4 (February 25, 1941). This, as well as the Rugg texts themselves, have been

major sources for my reconstruction of the Rugg controversy in Turin. Here is a quote from *Propaganda Analysis* (p. 7) that describes the controversy:

> Probably the hardest attack of the early months of the current fight, in 1939, was that of the American Federation of Advertisers. This was based at first on the treatment of advertising in Dr. Rugg's *Introduction to the Problems of American Culture.* It was quickly taken up by other advertising groups and by the bulletin of the American Newspaper Publishers Association. Then the attack was broadened and the whole Rugg series came to be condemned as subversive. The basis for this view was laid in a report by Alfred R. Falk, director of the Advertising Federation's Bureau of Research and Education, called "The Rugg Technique of Indoctrination." The report examined Dr. Rugg's philosophy of social reconstruction as expressed in his adult discussion book, *The Great Technology.*
>
> "This fantastic panacea," Mr. Falk says, "attempts to graft the tenets of technocracy upon a framework of Marxian socialism." Taking Dr. Rugg's statement that "a new public mind is to be created," Mr. Falk attempted to show that the textbooks worked toward this end by an "approach . . . of stealth." There are four steps in the Rugg indoctrination, Mr. Falk says. "First, the child is taught the great principle of Change—everything is in a constant state of change and we must expect all institutions to be changed in the future, especially forms of government and social organization. Second, the student is shown by numerous examples of factual and fictitious evidence that our present situation in this country is very unsatisfactory and our system has worked badly. Third, the child is disillusioned of any preconceived ideas that America has a glorious history or that the founding fathers were men of good intent. Rather, it is shown that our form of society was designed to benefit only the minority ruling class. Fourth, the panacea of social reconstruction and collectivist planning is advanced as the inevitable coming change.
>
> As one of Rugg's "unrepresentative examples," Mr. Falk quotes this passage from the textbook, *Conquests of America* (p. 540), in a reference to mill wages: "These people did not want to go to the towns to work in factories because the wages there were poor indeed—fifty hours a week for $5 . . ."

23. Scott, Hill, and Burns, eds., *The Great Debate* (1959), p. 57.

BIBLIOGRAPHY

Background for the history of education in Turin as well as for many of the ideas expressed throughout the book emerged from reading and research on our educational past that I've been doing over the last ten years. Without the help of Cynthia Brown, with her love of libraries and intuition about the location of original sources, the historical work on this book would not have been possible. And without the generous donation by Louis Laub of two hundred volumes of American educational classics to the Coastal Ridge Center, where I work, it would have been impossible for me to have immediate access to historical sources and to be able to reread, cross-reference, and internalize aspects of educational history. In particular, the donation of the United States Commissioner of Education's reports from 1876 to 1901 as well as the proceedings of the National Education Association from 1923 to 1951 were invaluable sources of educational thought and debate. Paul Monroe's five-volume *Cyclopedia of Education* (published by Macmillan from 1910 to 1914) was another major source that I relied on. In fact, it was by reading the article on Ohio Education in the Cyclopedia that I discovered Calvon Stowe and Henry Beecher's work on Cincinnati.

Another book that was a central source of information and leads is entitled *First Century of National Existence: The United States as They Were and Are. First Century* was complied, as the front page indicates, by "an eminent Corps of Scientific and Literary Men" and published by L. Stebbins of Hartford, Connecticut, in 1872. The book is a celebration of, and reflection on, the first hundred years of our national existence. The section on education, which is over one hundred double-column pages long, was written by Henry Barnard, who was to become the first United States Commissioner of Education. In compiling his information on one hundred years of education in the United States, Barnard sent out requests to over one hundred prominent educators and scholars that they write him about their own educational experiences and their feelings about progress in public education. The responses from people ranging from Noah Webster to Peter Parley (who wrote the first illustrated geography book) are lively and personal and convey a sense of struggle for public education from 1800 to 1872.

These sources, as well as Lawrence Cremin's *Transformation of the Schools*, led me to many other sources as I followed footnoted references or names or events mentioned casually.

Here is the bibliography of my sources:

Ayres, Leonard P. *The Cleveland School Survey.* 26 vols. Cleveland: The Survey Committee of the Cleveland Foundation, 1915–1917.

Bailyn, Bernard. *Education in the Forming of American Society.* New York: Vintage Books, 1960.

Ballard, Philip Boswood. *The Changing School.* London: Hodder and Stoughton, 1926.

Berkeley Citizens' Masterplan Facilities Committee, Berkeley Unified School District (June 15, 1978).

Bowen, Catherine Drinker. *The Most Dangerous Man in America.* Boston: Atlantic-Little, Brown, 1974.

——. *Writing of Biography.* Boston: The Writer, 1951.

Bowers, C. A. *The Progressive Educator and the Depression.* New York: Random House, 1969.

Branan, Karen, and Joe Nathan. "Students as Consumer Advocates." *Learning Magazine* (March 1977).

Charters, W. W. "The Project Method of Learning." *Journal of Home Economics* 10 (March 1918): 168-178.

Cobb, Stanwood. *The New Leaven: Progressive Education and Its Effect upon the Child and Society.* New York: Arno Press and the *New York Times*, 1969. Originally published in New York by the John Day Company in 1932.

Cremin, Lawrence A. *Public Education.* New York: Basic Books, 1976.

——. *Traditions of American Education.* New York: Basic Books, 1977.

——. *The Transformation of the School: Progressivism in American Education, 1876–1957.* New York: Alfred A. Knopf, 1961.

De Guimps, Roger. *Pestalozzi: His Life and Work.* International Education Series. New York: D. Appleton and Company, 1894.

De Koven, Bernard. *The Well-Played Game.* New York: Doubleday, 1978.

Dennison, George. *The Lives of Children.* New York: Bantam Books. 1968.

Dewey, John. *The Child and the Curriculum and the School and Society.* Chicago and London: The University of Chicago Press, 1971.

———. *Education Today*, ed. Joseph Ratner. New York: G. P. Putnam's Sons, 1940.

———. *Experience and Education*. The Kappa Delta Pi Lecture Series. New York: Collier Books, 1963.

———. *John Dewey on Education: Selected Writings*. ed. Reginald D. Archambault. Chicago and London: The University of Chicago Press, Phoenix Books, 1974.

———. *My Pedagogic Creed*; and Albion W. Small. *The Demands of Sociology Upon Pedagogy*. Chicago: A. Flanagan Company, 1897.

———. *The School and Society*, rev. ed. Chicago: The University of Chicago Press, 1926.

Dewey, John, and Evelyn Dewey. *Schools of Tomorrow*. New York: E. P. Dutton and Company, 1915.

Dewey, John, and James A. McLellan. *The Psychology of Number, and Its Applications to Methods of Teaching Artihmetic*. International Education Series. New York: D. Appleton and Company, 1896.

Dropkin, Ruth, and Arthur Tabier, eds. *Roots of Open Education in America*. New York: The City College Workshop for Open Education, December 1976.

DuBois, W. E. B. *Crisis* 40 (1925).

First Century of National Existence: The United States as They Were and Are. Selected subjects and authors. Hartford, CT: L. Stebbins, 1872.

Franklin, Benjamin. *Proposals Relating to the Education of Youth in Pennsylvania*. Published in Philadelphia, 1749.

Goodman, Paul. *Compulsory Mis-Education and the Community of Scholars*. New York: Vintage Books, 1966.

Gross, Ronald. *The Lifelong Learner*. New York: Simon & Schuster, 1977.

Hall, G. Stanely. *Aspects of Child Life and Education*, ed. Theodate L. Smith. Boston: Ginn and Company, 1907.

———. *Educational Problems*, vos. 1 and 2. New York: D. Appleton and Company, 1924.

Harty, Shiela. *Hucksters in the Classroom: A Review of Industry Propaganda in the Schools*. Washington, DC: Center for Study of Responsive Law, 1979.

Herndon, James. *In Your Native Land*. New York: Bantam Books, 1972.

———. *The Way It Spozed to Be*. New York: Bantam Books, 1969.

Holt, John. *How Children Fail*. New York: Pitman Publishing Company, 1964.

———. *How Children Learn*. New York: Pitman Publishing Company, 1967.

Hubbard, Elbert. *Little Journeys to the Homes of Great Teachers: Friedrich Froebel*. New York: The Roycrofters, 1908.

Jacks, L. P. *The Education of the Whole Man*. New York: Harper and Brothers, 1931.

Johnson, Marietta. *Thirty Years With an Idea*. University, AL: The University of Alabama Press, 1974.

Kozol, Jonathan. *Death at an Early Age*. New York: Bantam Books, 1968.

Lopate, Phillip. *Journal of a Living Experiment: A Documentary History of the First Ten Years of Teachers and Writers Collaborative.* New York: Teachers and Writers Collaborative, 84 Fifth Avenue, New York, New York 10011.

Mann, Mary Peabody. *Life of Horace Mann.* Washington, DC: National Education Association of the United States, 1937. Centennial Edition in Facsimile, reproduced from original edition published in Boston by Walker, Fuller and Company, 1865.

Marshall, Sybil. *An Experiment in Education.* Cambridge: Cambridge University Press, 1963.

McCaul, Robert L. "Dewey's Chicago." *The School Review* (Summer 1959): 258–81.

Miller, Lida Brooks. *The Kindergarten, or, Home and School Culture.* Chicago: National Publishing Company, 1891.

Monroe, Paul. *A Cyclopedia of Education,* vos. 1–5. New York: Macmillan, 1911.

——, ed. *Principles of Secondary Education.* New York: Macmillan, 1914.

Monroe, Walter Scott. *An Introduction to the Theory of Educational Measurements.* Boston: Houghton Mifflin, 1923.

Monroe, Will S. *The Educational Labors of Henry Barnard: A Study in the History of American Pedagogy.* Syracuse, NY: C. W. Bardeen, 1893.

Mortenson, Enok. *Schools for Life.* Solvang, CA: Danish-American Heritage Society, 1977.

Nearing, Scott. *The New Education: A Review of Progressive Educational Movements of the Day.* Chicago and New York: Row, Peterson and Company, 1915.

Norris School Cooperative Program. *Adult Education* 10, no. 4 (June 1838).

North Dakota Study Group on Evaluation. *Reading Tests: Do They Help or Hurt Your Child.* Grand Forks: University of North Dakota, Center for Teaching and Learning. This booklet and other valuable inexpensive material on the problems of standardized testing can be ordered from the Study Group or from Ann Cook and Deborah Meier, 670 West End Avenue, New York, NY 10025.

Parker, Francis W. *Talks on Pedagogics.* New York: Arno Press and the *New York Times,* 1969. Originally published in New York by E. L. Kellogg and Company, 1894.

Patri, Angelo. *A Schoolmaster of the Great City.* New York: Macmillan, 1923.

Pestalozzi, Heinrich. *The Education of Man: Aphorisms,* trans. Heinz and Ruth Norden. New York: Philosophical Library, 1951.

——. *Leornard and Gertrude.* Translated and abridged by Eva Channing. Boston: D. C. Heath, 1895.

Pinloche, A. *Pestalozzi and the Foundation of the Modern Elementary School.* The Great Educators series. New York: Charles Scribner's Sons, 1912.

Pintner, Rudolf. *Intelligence Testing: Methods and Results.* New York: Henry Holt and Company, 1924.

Pressey, Sidney L., and Luella Cole Pressey, *Introduction to the Use of Standard Tests: A Brief Manual in the Use of Tests of Both Ability and Achievement in the*

School Subjects. New York: World Book Company, 1922.

Proceedings of the NEA meeting in Oakland, California, 1923.

Proctor, William Martin. "The Use of Psychological Tests in the Educational and Vocational Guidance of High School Pupils. Journal of Eduational Research Monographs," no. 1. Bloomington, IL: Public School Publishing Company, 1921.

Propaganda Analysis 4, no. 4 (February 25, 1941).

Rice, Joseph Mayer. *The Public School System of the United States*. New York: 1893.

Rousseau, Jean Jacques. *Emile*, trans. Barbara Foxley. London: J. M. Dent and Sons, 1955. First published in 1911.

Rugg, Harold. *America's March Toward Democracy, History of American Life: Political and Social*. Boston: Ginn and Company, 1937.

Rugg, Harold. *Curriculum-Making, Past and Present*. New York: Arno Press and the *New York Times*, 1969. American Education Series. Originally published in Bloomington, IL, by the Public School Publishing Company, 1926.

Rugg, Harold et al. *The Foundation of Curriculum-Making*. New York: Arno Press and the *New York Times*, 1969. Originally published in Bloomington, IL, by the Public School Publishing Company, 1926.

Rugg, Harold, and Louise Krueger. *Communities of Men*. New York: Ginn and Company, 1936.

Rugg, Harold, and Ann Shumaker. *The Child-Centered School*. New York: Arno Press and the *New York Times*, 1969. American Education Series. Originally published in New York by World Book Company, 1928.

Scott, C. Winfield, Clyde M. Hill, and Hobert W. Burns, eds. *The Great Debate*. Englewood Cliffs, NJ: Prentice-Hall, 1959.

Shragg, Peter, and Diane Divoki. *The Myth of the Hyperactive Child*. New York: Dell, 1976.

Smith, William Hawley. *All of the Children of All of the People*. New York: Macmillan, 1912.

Stonorov, Oscar, and Louis Kahn. *You and Your Community: A Primer*. Published as a public service by Revere Copper and Brass, Inc., 1944.

Stowe, Calvin. *The Report on Elementary Public Instruction in Europe*. Columbus: The Ohio State Legislature, 1837.

Synnott, Marcia G. "The Admission and Arsenal of Minority Students at Harvard, Yale and Princeton 1900–1950." *Journal of the History of Eduation* 19, no. 3 (Fall 1979).

Terman, Lewis M. *The Intelligence of School Children, How Children Differ in Ability, The Use of Mental Tests in School Grading, and the Proper Education of Exceptional Children*. Boston: Houghton Mifflin, 1919.

——. *The Measurement of Intelligence, An Explanation of and a Complete Guide for the Use of the Stanford Revision and Extension of the Binet-Simon Intelligence Scale*. Boston: Houghton Mifflin, 1916.

Terman, Lewis M., et al. *Intelligence Tests and School Reorganization.* New York: World Book Company, 1922.

Thorndike, Edward L. *Handwriting.* New York: Teachers College, Columbia University, 1917.

———. *The Principles of Teaching, Based on Psychology.* New York: A. G. Seiler, 1906.

Von Marenholz-Bulow, Baroness B. *Reminiscences of Friedrich Froebel,* trans. Mrs. Horace Mann. Boston: Lee and Shepard, 1877.

Wallace, F. C. *Rockdale.* New York: Knopf, 1978.

Wesker, Arnold. *Words as Definitions of Experience.* London: Writers and Readers Publishing Company, 1976.

Woodham-Smith, P., et al. *Friedrich Froebel and English Education,* ed. Evelyn Lawrence. London: University of London Press, 1961. First published 1952.

Woodhull, John F. "The Aims and Methods of Science Teaching." *General Science Quarterly* 2 (November 1917) : 249.